PRAISE FOR *THE KING IS COMING*

Here is a healthy dose of sanity on the study of prophecy. My friend Erwin Lutzer writes from long hours of informed study and presents essential truths with compelling clarity. He navigates our reading boat away from the rocks of sensationalism on the one side and complacency on the other, guiding us to listen well to God's prophetic Word.

—**MARK L. BAILEY,** *president, Dallas Theological Seminary*

There are peacekeepers and there are truth tellers. I have always found Erwin Lutzer to be the latter, whether in his powerful preaching, incisive teaching, or dynamic writing. You'll find *The King Is Coming* represents the best of one of evangelicalism's most persuasive thinkers on a topic crucial to all.

—**JERRY B. JENKINS,** *novelist and biographer; owner, Christian Writers Guild*

In a day when people are starved for an answer about the end of the world and the second coming, Erwin Lutzer answers with a biblical, expositional, rational, thoughtful book on the coming of Christ. Here you will find rare insight from God's Word by one of today's most scholarly pastors.

—**MAC BRUNSON,** *senior pastor, First Baptist Church, Jacksonville, Florida*

What a clear picture of prophecy and its practical relevance for our lives today! Dr. Lutzer is compelling in his reminder that we as Christians will all stand at the judgment seat of Christ to give an account for how we've lived. If we understood this sobering truth, it would change the way we live *now*.

—**KAY ARTHUR,** *cofounder, Precept Ministries International*

Finally! With fresh observation and clarifying exposition, Erwin Lutzer has taken difficult prophetic issues and placed them within our reach. But he isn't satisfied to simply provide biblical answers about the world of tomorrow; he's passionate in preparing us to walk wisely in our world today.

—**STEPHEN DAVEY,** *pastor/teacher, Colonial Baptist Church, Cary, North Carolina; president, Shepherds Theological Seminary*

I recommend this book for believers looking for a resource to help unbelieving friends gain perspective on the prospect of eternity.

—**JOHN JELINEK,** *vice president and academic dean, Moody Theological Seminary*

The King Is Coming: what a great title and what a great promise! The Bible predicts many things about the future, but the most important prophecy of all is the promise that Jesus is coming again. Don't miss Dr. Lutzer's insightful, captivating, and provocative new book. It will stir your soul and bless your heart.

—**ED HINDSON,** *distinguished professor, School of Religion, Liberty University*

Erwin Lutzer has done a masterful job of presenting what Billy Graham has called the most neglected doctrine of our faith: the second coming of Jesus Christ. Dr. Lutzer avoids getting bogged down in the peripheral issues of eschatology and focuses on how the certainty of Christ's return should affect our lives today. This hope-filled book is must reading for every believer.

—**ROBERT JEFFRESS,** *pastor, First Baptist Church, Dallas*

Imagine! A book on prophecy whose primary purpose is not to satisfy our curiosity but to change our lives by motivating us to live in light of the Lord's return. My friend Erwin Lutzer has written a book that will inform you, bless you, and remind you that time is short and eternity will soon begin.

—**JAMES MEEKS,** *pastor, Salem Baptist Church of Chicago*

Lutzer presents the book of Revelation with the mind of a scholar and the heart of a pastor. Regardless of your view of the end times, these words will challenge, equip, and inspire you to deeper devotion to Christ and a life that longs for His coming. This is a book both to read and to savor as you seek to understand God's plan for the last days.

—**JOHN ANKERBERG,** *founder and president,* The John Ankerberg Show

THE KING
IS COMING

ERWIN W. LUTZER

THE KING
IS COMING

TEN EVENTS THAT WILL
CHANGE OUR FUTURE FOREVER

MOODY PUBLISHERS

CHICAGO

All Scripture quotations, unless otherwise indicated, are taken from the *Holy Bible, New International Version*®, NIV®. Copyright ©1973, 1978, 1984 by Biblica, Inc.™ Used by permission of Zondervan. All rights reserved worldwide. www.zondervan .com.

Scripture quotations marked ESV are taken from *The Holy Bible, English Standard Version*. Copyright © 2000, 2001 by Crossway Bibles, a division of Good News Publishers. Used by permission. All rights reserved.

Scripture quotations marked KJV are taken from the King James Version.

Edited by Elizabeth Cody Newenhuyse
Interior design: Puckett Smartt
Cover design: Geoffrey Sciacca
Cover photo: Eric Gevaert / iStock

Library of Congress Cataloging-in-Publication Data
Lutzer, Erwin W.
 The King is coming : ten events that will change our future forever /
Erwin W. Lutzer.
   p. cm.
Includes bibliographical references.
ISBN 978-0-8024-1287-4
1. Second Advent--Biblical teaching. 2. End of the world--Biblical
teaching. I. Title.
BT886.3.L88 2012
236'.9--dc23
                    2012006507

CONTENTS

FOREWORD

"The end of the world is coming!" These are not merely words on a sign held by a disheveled protester. A major motion picture predicted the end of the world in 2012, basing its message on the ancient Mayan calendar. A radio preacher predicted the actual date of Jesus' return but got it wrong . . . twice. It seems that interest in the end of days waxes and wanes, depending on the most recent news in the Middle East. Heightened tensions bring increased interest while periods of relative calm shove thoughts of the end to the back burner. This is why I so welcome *The King Is Coming* by Pastor Erwin Lutzer—it is a book about the end that will not lead people astray. Here is why:

First, this book uses the right source for understanding the end of days. The answers to the world's questions are not to be found in ancient calendars or enigmatic calculations but in God's Word, the Bible. It alone is the authoritative revelation of God. Nothing but the Bible can tell what will happen in the future. And when the Bible makes predictions, we can depend on its absolute dependability.

Second, this book has a reasonable approach to Bible prophecy. It is not sensational, finding obscure meanings in hidden verses. It does not base its interpretations on newspaper articles or cable TV reports. Rather, it offers sound, sensible, balanced perspectives based on the simple literary meaning of ancient biblical texts. Avoiding fruitless speculation and careless projections, Pastor Lutzer, using the Bible, details what can be known about the future of the world.

Third, this book is driven by the best motive for reading Bible prophecy. It is not designed to tickle our curiosity or to inflame our fears, but is based on the biblical principle found in 1 John 3:2–3: "We know that when He appears, we will be like Him, because we will see Him just as He is. And everyone who has this hope fixed on Him purifies himself, just as He is pure." The purpose of this book is to renew our expectation of the return of the Messiah Jesus and, in so doing, motivate us to live pure lives for Him. This holy purpose is the reason that more than half of God's Word is prophetic. Pastor Lutzer reminds us that as we await our Redeemer's return, we must live faithful and pure lives for Him.

Yes, we need a biblically accurate, sane, and sanctifying book about Bible prophecy. And no author and Bible teacher is more qualified to write it than my pastor and friend, Erwin Lutzer. His love for Jesus and His appearing is great; his knowledge of God's Word is deep; his skill at communication is immense; and his wisdom in applying God's truth is profound. Applying these unique traits to a book of Bible prophecy has produced a work of great value and life transforming truth.

I challenge you to read this book as an active student. Read it carefully and prayerfully. Use a highlighter, mark in its margins; take notes. And when you are done you will find your hope restored and your longing for His appearing renewed.

Dr. Michael Rydelnik
Professor of Jewish Studies
Moody Bible Institute

WELCOME TO
YOUR FUTURE

The King is coming!

But how do we know—and what does that mean for you?

Whether you will be present when the unimaginable happens is not your choice. Whether the return of Jesus will be a blessed experience of happiness or the beginning of an eternity of horror—either way, you will be involved in these events. If you are still alive when Jesus returns, you will either be caught up to be with Him, or you will be left behind to suffer personal grief and tribulation. And if you are a believer in Christ but already dead when He returns to wrap up history as we know it, you will immediately be raised to everlasting life; if not, you will be raised from the dead at a later time to face everlasting damnation.

The bottom line: Let me paraphrase C. S. Lewis and say we are eternal beings, destined for either unimaginable glory or unimaginable horror. Either way, we cannot escape the future that will someday unfold. Preparing for our eternal future should be our highest priority.

To do so, we must understand what the Bible says about these glorious—and terrifying—events. We must come to grips with prophecy.

THE PROBLEM OF PROPHECY

There are several reasons why prophecy has a bad reputation today. The first is due to many false predictions by well-meaning but misguided souls. I'm not simply talking about people who gather on a hilltop believing that Jesus is going to come at midnight on a certain day. Yes, there have been prophecy teachers who convince their flock to sell all they have because the Lord's return is at hand. And many dear people—God have mercy on them—with inexplicable gullibility are willing to obey their teacher. When the Lord doesn't return on the specified date, they have virtually lost all they had in this life and cannot recoup their losses. What an embarrassment to the watching world.

My concern is not only with such foolishness, however. I'm thinking about well-known Bible preachers, and otherwise excellent teachers, who have carefully looked at the Scriptures and then made predictions regarding how many years remain or that "we're very close to midnight," yet somehow midnight never comes. Years ago at the Moody Bible Institute library I checked out a book written by a noted Christian leader who is in heaven today. He wrote a book in the 1940s to show that Hitler was the Antichrist and that Mussolini was the false prophet. The case was compelling, but there was one problem. He was wrong.

Yes, I acknowledge that world events appear to be shaping up for the return of Christ. For example, since Antichrist is going to use economics to rule the globe, our present economic crisis could indeed usher in a worldwide economic collapse that would force the world to accept an "economic tsar" to bring hope and stability to a world run amok. Already, as we shall see later, just as Hitler arose as a result of economic decline and chaos, just so Antichrist shall seize his opportunity to restore financial sanity and "economic equality." But we simply don't know who the Antichrist might be or whether he is alive today. We must humbly confess that we don't know exactly how and when God will wrap up history.

The same can be said for the geopolitical events of the Middle East. We know that Israel must be in the land in order for all of the promises God gave to Abraham to be fulfilled. Today, Israel is in her land, but we do not know all that must take place before the Lord returns to the Mount of Olives as Zechariah prophesied. Those who predicted back in 1948 that the Lord would return within the next few years now that the Jewish nation had been formed, were of course, wrong in their assumptions. It is possible to be right about the facts but very wrong about the timeline.

> WHY CAN'T WE GET EVERYBODY IN THE SAME ROOM WITH THE SAME BIBLE AND THEN COME UP WITH A CHART THAT WE CAN ALL RELY UPON?

Certainly there are other signs of Christ's return that we shall note in passing, but I'd like this book to remain relevant even if Jesus doesn't come in the next ten years, or the next twenty years, or beyond. I want to share with you the ten events we know will happen even though the time frame is unknown to us. In answer to the question, "How close are we to the Lord's return?" the best answer always is, "a day closer than we were yesterday!"

There is a second reason why people today are skeptical about prophecy. It's controversial. Will Jesus come before, during, or after the tribulation? Will there be a literal millennial kingdom on earth or is this kingdom going to be realized in heaven? Or are we already in the kingdom age? Perhaps you wonder why

Bible teachers can't agree on these issues. Why can't we get all the scholars in the same room with the same Bible and then come up with a chart that we can all rely upon?

The reason that such agreement is difficult is because the Bible tells us *what* will happen but it doesn't provide all of the sequences. Teaching on prophecy is found in various parts of the Old and New Testaments, and is not presented in one place in a coherent whole. The Bible leaves it to us to gather all the various teachings about prophecy and then painstakingly put the pieces together in a sequence so that everything "fits together." So it is understandable that experts would disagree on which sequences work best. As a friend of mine says, it is like putting a puzzle together without a picture on the box.

Another problem is that some Bible students take certain Scriptures more literally than others, leading to different conclusions regarding important details of the end times. Are the locusts in Revelation really locusts, military helicopters, or symbolic of something else? Does the church replace Israel in God's prophetic scheme or are there still promises God made to the nation of Israel that must be fulfilled? When the prophets spoke of a kingdom of peace yet to come, is this a description of heaven, or will these predictions actually still take place on the earth? These are important questions, and even the best prophecy researchers disagree on how literally particular verses are taken.

However—and this is important—regardless of one's view of end time events, the Bible repeatedly teaches the visible, literal return of Jesus back to earth. It teaches the personal judgment of all individuals; it teaches an eternal heaven and an eternal hell. We don't have to be right about all the details in order for prophecy to change our entire perspective on life; we don't have to agree on everything to look forward to the return of Jesus as the Bible says we should do.

Here I must offer a comment on some popular "prophecies" that have been making the rounds recently. The contrast between Bible prophecy and mystical New Age prophecies is striking. Hollywood is only too glad to enter the fray and produce movies that spell the end of the world as we know it. We are all acquainted with the hype about the Mayan calendar and its prediction of doomsday. The movie, *2012*, in typical Hollywood style, used some facts about the Mayan calendar and added tantalizing fiction and dramatic sound effects to describe the utter destruction of the earth along with human societies. But scholars are not even agreed that the so-called "Long Count" calendar that these events claim to be based on actually predicts the end of the world, nor can we be sure that the date was to have been 2012. Satan might try to bring about some events to convince the world that these prophecies are legitimate, but the "fulfillment" is ambiguous, subject to a variety of interpretations.

Remember that human prophecies (such as the Mayan calendar) and occult prophecies (such as Nostradamus) are always nonspecific; to predict the end of the earth is easy enough, but to give details is quite different. Such prophecies are always disguised in ambiguity and are subject to numerous interpretations. For example, not a single event could ever have been predicted by anyone who read the writings of Nostradamus. It is only *after* various events have occurred that admirers have used their imaginations and ingenuity to find these events in his writings. It is so much easier to wait for an event to have happened and then find it in some obscure prophetic writing, than to actually predict the event *before* it happens!

How different are the prophecies of the Bible! As we shall discover in our study, here nations are named, geographical locations are described and existing mountains and lakes are referred to. Antichrist is not only described but the speeches he will eventually give are summarized for us; Jesus is not only predicted to return but He is to descend to the Mount of Olives just east of Jerusalem. When we open the pages of the Bible we are not left to our imaginations to try to interpret the vague musings of an occultist, nor the confusing intention of a cyclical calendar.

How sure can we be that Christ will return to earth? As sure as we are that He came to this earth as a baby in Bethlehem, suffered, died, and was raised from His grave. Keep in mind that there was a time when the death and resurrection of Jesus was prophecy. Today, of course, it is history. Just so, the return of Christ is prophecy today but it will be history at some future date. The fact that He is coming is just as certain as the fact that He already came! All true prophecies eventually become true history.

THE MOST IMPORTANT REASON TO STUDY PROPHECY

In these pages, you will be introduced to some of these controversies but it is not my intention to prove one view over another, or to spend a lot of time trying to argue a particular detail regarding the road map of Bible prophecy. I will make some basic assumptions and give reasons for what I believe, but my goal is to provide an overview of the ten events that I believe must take place according to the Bible. I am convinced that these events will happen even if, when Jesus returns, we discover that our sequence may have needed some adjustment. Whether or not every interpretation is correct, the full force of the prophetic Scriptures must be considered. We cannot let disagreements stand in the way of looking forward to Christ's return and ordering our lives accordingly.

MY DESIRE IS FOR YOU TO FALL IN LOVE WITH JESUS ALL OVER AGAIN.

My desire is for you to fall in love with Jesus all over again. The apostle Paul said, "It is time for me to be offered." That is, "It is time for me to die." In his final letter, Paul shared with young

Timothy, "I have fought a good fight, I have kept the faith, therefore there is laid up for me a crown of righteousness which the Lord, the righteous judge, shall give me on that day, and not to me only, but to all them also who love his appearing" (2 Timothy 4:7–8). As a result of these studies, I want you to love His appearing, just like Paul did, and just like Scripture invites us to.

And so the final reason for this book is, of course, to be ready to meet King Jesus. John said that we should live in such a way as to not shrink with shame at His coming (1 John 2:28). The clear implication is that some Christians are going to be ashamed in the presence of Jesus. When we will think back to how we lived in light of God's promises and the opportunities He has given us . . . well might we be ashamed. Let us resolve today to live in light of Christ's return and not fear seeing Him—but let us long to be in His very presence.

And what if we live a life of anticipation and faithfulness yet Jesus does not return in our lifetime? We have lost nothing, because those who die before Christ comes have no disadvantage. Whether we are living when Christ comes or whether we will have already died, either way, we shall all stand in the presence of Christ to give an account for the way we lived; we shall all experience the joys of the New Jerusalem together, and have uninterrupted fellowship with God. As we study these events, we will be humbled to realize that we all will be a part of the unfolding of God's eternal plan.

I pray that all who read this book will understand why they must trust Christ as Savior if they wish to be spared from "the coming wrath" (1 Thessalonians 1:10). The sorrows of the great tribulation and the horrors of the great white throne judgment should be sufficient to motivate all of us to make certain that our faith is in Christ, the Savior who came to deliver us from eternal condemnation. There can be no greater contrast than the glory of the saints and the suffering of unredeemed sinners.

The apostle Peter wrote, "Since everything will be destroyed in this way, what kind of people ought you to be? You ought to live holy and godly lives" (2 Peter 3:11). The goal of this study in biblical prophecy is to change our lives, moving from the pursuit of happiness to the pursuit of holiness and from the love of the world to the love of God. You'll be hearing me repeat this simple phrase: *time is short and eternity is long.*

Think of the wisdom of living for the "forever after"!

DEFINING THE TERMS

As we begin, it is important to understand a few prophetic terms related to Bible prophecy. First, there is the teaching known as *pretribulationism* ("before the tribulation"), the view that the return of Jesus Christ will take place in two stages. First, Jesus will come for His church (that is all those who have trusted in Christ since the church began on the day of Pentecost). This means that at the rapture, all living Christians will be taken to heaven, and the "dead in Christ" will rise before the seven-year tribulation yet to come. At the end of the seven years, the second stage of His return will take place, and Jesus will return and establish His kingdom. In the first coming, He comes *for* His saints. The next time He appears, it is *with* His saints. The point, of course, is that all Christians are in heaven during the great tribulation on earth.

Another view, known as *prewrath*, holds that the return of Christ for His church occurs in the midpoint of the tribulation. Believers suffer for the first three and one-half years under the hands of men, and only then does the Lord return to take them to heaven. After the rapture, the wrath of God is poured onto the earth for the last three and one-half years. Since this view also holds that the coming of Jesus is in two stages, it has many similarities to pretribulationism, but differs only in the length of time between the two comings.

Posttribulationism, however, teaches that Jesus has only one appearing when He returns on earth, and this event will be *after* the tribulation. Also, it follows that according to this view, all believers living at that time will have to experience the terrors of the great tribulation. Following this seven-year tribulation, which will include a global world ruler called the Antichrist, Jesus will then come to receive the then-living members of the church and immediately establish His kingdom. So according to this view, the rapture of "the dead in Christ" and the glorious appearing of Christ take place simultaneously.

There has been much debate among many godly people concerning all of these positions. For our purposes, I will assume the pretribulation rapture of the church; that is, the coming of Jesus for His church will take place before the tribulation begins. I believe that if we as followers of Christ are alive when Jesus comes, we will be caught up into heaven and escape the tribulation; and then at a later time Christ will bring us with Him in a glorious appearing to establish His kingdom. As we shall learn, the more literally we take the predictions, the more clearly we will see the church as a distinct body to be differentiated from Israel, and hence the church will be taken out of the way before Jesus returns to judge the world and prepare Israel for the coming kingdom.

Two other terms will become important later in this book. *Premillennialism* ("before the millennium") teaches that this is not the kingdom age, but when Jesus returns to earth in a blaze of glory, He will establish His kingdom here on earth. That word *millennium* literally means "a thousand" and is used to describe the scene in Revelation chapter 20, where Christ and His followers are found to reign for a thousand years. In fact, that phrase occurs six times in this one chapter. Therefore, we refer to "the millennial kingdom."

Another term, *amillennialism*, teaches that there is no earthly kingdom to come. Those who follow this view say that the Old Testament prophecies of the kingdom are either (1) being fulfilled in heaven today or (2) that the church is the kingdom, so there is no future rule of Christ on earth. In other words, the church has replaced Israel in God's scheme, and therefore the promises about the regathering of Israel and the establishment of an earthly kingdom are reinterpreted. This view is often referred to as "replacement theology."

The viewpoint in this book is that of *premillennialism*, which, as we've seen, holds to the belief that Christ will establish a future kingdom after He returns to earth. This means that the prophecies originally given to the nation Israel will yet be fulfilled for the nation Israel. Although the church inherits many of the prophecies given to Israel, it does not inherit all of them. Prophecies about the land, the throne of David, and a kingdom of peace are yet to be fulfilled by King Jesus right here on this planet.

Enough about definitions. Let's begin our journey as we think about the ten events that the Scriptures teach are still to take place. Let's ask God to help us understand these descriptions not merely as doctrines but as life-changing transitions that we are certain will take place. Let God redirect our lives by contemplating these momentous events in which we will be involved.

"Even so, come, Lord Jesus"!

CHAPTER ONE

THE KING
RETURNS FOR US

*When we put our trust in Jesus Christ, we transfer from the
road to Armagedon to the road to Glory.*
—John Walvoord

Imagine you are having a regular day at home or at the office,
and then without warning, you are in the presence of Christ
with a new body and in an entirely different realm of existence.
Incredibly, Jesus is there; friends who have died and gone to
heaven are there; and you find yourself mingling with an innu-
merable host of people, all suspended in midair. You are reunited
with your mother, father, and friends long since forgotten on
earth. But the focus is on your leader, Savior, King Jesus, who returned as He promised. "And if I go and prepare a place for you, I
will come back and take you to be with me that you also may be
where I am" (John 14:3).

WHY DOES THIS MATTER?

For many of us the return of Jesus often seems theoretical, far off, and quite irrelevant to our daily existence. We think that prophecy is a scheme to be understood by mature Christians— but recent converts (we believe) need other kinds of doctrine. After all, Christ has not returned in the last two thousand years and He might not return before the next thousand years have expired. So, we surmise, let the return of Christ be the last topic to be studied and grasped. Looking for Christ's return is a wonderful ideal, but practical people have other matters to worry about.

> FOR MANY OF US THE RETURN OF JESUS OFTEN SEEMS THEORETICAL, FAR OFF, AND QUITE IRRELEVANT TO OUR DAILY EXISTENCE.

But Paul the apostle strongly disagreed with the notion that the study of prophecy should be left for the curious-minded folk who are so "heavenly minded" that they lack the practicality of how to live on earth. He did not intend that the events that surround the return of Jesus just be investigated by "prophecy buffs" who spend time wondering if they know who the Antichrist is or whether the European Union is the fulfillment of Daniel's prophecy. Don't misunderstand, these topics are all relevant, but if we are sidetracked by such discussions we might miss the very purpose of why prophecy was given to us. *Prophecy is intended for every believer because the return of Jesus is to be our focus and hope.*

When Paul began a church, filled with new believers, he taught them about the return of Jesus. For this church planter, prophecy was the heartbeat of his life and ministry. So we should not be surprised that when he founded the church in Thessalonica he taught them to look forward to Christ's return. He knew that a focus on the return of Christ would keep the congregation pure and courageous. But, as all prophecy teachers have learned, people are often confused about the details, and sometimes even

Paul left his students with more questions than answers.

The believers in the church looked forward to the return of Christ in their lifetime, but obviously, He did not return and so some Christians were confused about what would happen to them if they died before He returned. Some of their friends died, so they were wondering, "Our friends who died before Christ's return, are they at a disadvantage? What about my uncle? What about my wife, my husband, my child? Will they miss the return of Jesus if and when He comes for those of us who are living?"

Paul's answer, as we shall see, is a resounding no. He taught them that their loved ones will not be at a disadvantage. In fact, the dead will rise even before the living are caught away into heaven. Both the dead and the living will be transformed at almost the same time; they will be given new bodies and a new home. All that in "the twinkling of an eye" (1 Corinthians 15:52)!

PAUL'S WORDS OF COMFORT

So Paul answered the concerns of the believers in the church by introducing them to the details surrounding the rapture of the church, the "snatching away" of all the living believers when Christ returns. And, yes, the additional news is that those who have died will actually be raised a moment before the living are caught up to heaven. Just read the full context of Paul's comments in 1 Thessalonians 4:13–18:

> Brothers, we do not want you to be ignorant about those who fall asleep, or to grieve like the rest of men, who have no hope. We believe that Jesus died and rose again and so we believe that God will bring with Jesus those who have fallen asleep in him. According to the Lord's own word, we tell you that we who are still alive, who are left till the coming of the Lord, will certainly not precede

IT IS TRUE THAT ENGLISH TRANSLATIONS DO NOT INCLUDE THE WORD *RAPTURE*, BUT THE RAPTURE IS A THOROUGHLY BIBLICAL TERM.

those who have fallen asleep. For the Lord himself will come down from heaven, with a loud command, with the voice of the archangel and with the trumpet call of God, and the dead in Christ will rise first. After that, we who are still alive and are left will be caught up together with them in the clouds to meet the Lord in the air. And so we will be with the Lord forever. Therefore encourage each other with these words.

When I prepared to preach a message on the *rapture*, a friend said to me, "You're speaking on the rapture? The word 'rapture' doesn't even occur in the Bible!" Technically, in English this may be true, but take a moment to look back to the passage just quoted. "After that, we who are still alive and are left will be *caught up* together with them in the clouds to meet the Lord in the air. And so we will be with the Lord forever" (v. 17, italics added). The Latin word for "caught up" is *rapturo* from which we get the word *rapture*. So it is true that English translations do not include the word *rapture*, but the rapture is a thoroughly biblical term. The day is coming when living Christians will be "caught up" to be with the Lord and with each other forever.

Let's get the sequence of events in our minds:

BELIEVERS ARE WITH THE LORD

Paul taught that believers who die will immediately depart to be with God in heaven. In fact, several times he spoke of his own preference to die and be "with the Lord" (see 2 Corinthians 5:8; Philippians 1:21). My wife Rebecca and I were in Colorado Springs for the funeral of a dear friend who was a musician. He died unexpectedly in his sleep. His body was laid tenderly in the ground and even as we were there at his grave, his soul/spirit was already in the presence of God in heaven. There, I'm sure, his soul/spirit took on the characteristics of a body and he was able to communicate with Jesus and others who were already there. In heaven, Christians recognize one another; they are in the presence of Jesus, enjoying Him, but they are still incomplete. Their permanent resurrection bodies have not yet been given to them.

The wife of a friend of mine also died unexpectedly in her sleep. The widower, God bless him, is sorrowing intensely, anxiously awaiting the day when he will die to be reunited with the one he so dearly loves. We can understand that, but when a loved one dies, we should remember this: although we miss them, they would never want to return to earth even if they could. As a friend of mine said, *"No Christian who has ever died has regretted it!"* They have already seen Christ, they have been reunited with friends, they are free of sorrow and pain. Yes, they no doubt await our arrival, but having had a glimpse of eternity, they can only rejoice that we will soon be with them.

JESUS WILL RETURN WITH BELIEVERS WHO HAVE DIED

Next, the apostle Paul says that when Jesus comes in the rapture, He will bring with Him "the dead in Christ." The souls of all those who have died and are presently in heaven, all these will return with Christ. Take a moment to contemplate what this means. I think of my father who died at 106 years old; I think of my dear mother who died at 103; I think of other relatives and friends who are in heaven; children to whom we said goodbye, all of whom are already in heaven—these will return with Jesus.

Just imagine: all of these souls of the dead will be returning with Christ. These people are very much alive, having been in heaven since the time of the death of their bodies. And if I die before Christ returns, I also hope to return with that number! Jesus will bring with Him those who have "fallen asleep," an expression used in the New Testament to refer to all those who die as believers.

THE LORD WILL DESCEND WITH A SHOUT, "GET UP! YOU'VE BEEN DEAD LONG ENOUGH!"

Janet Willis, the mother of nine children, six of whom were killed in a tragic accident back in 1994, says that even amid her grief there are three things she knows about her precious children: "First, they are safe, second, they are good, and third, they are happy, and I will see them again!" What a testimony to the power of God's promises and the assurance that those who die in Christ are even now with the Lord. Yes, those children will be returning with Christ when He comes to receive His redeemed people.

ALL BELIEVERS RECEIVE NEW BODIES

The souls of the dead will now be joined to their newly resurrected bodies. "For the Lord himself will come down from heaven, with a loud command, with the voice of the archangel and with the trumpet call of God, and the dead in Christ will rise first" (1 Thessalonians 4:16). Amazing! If you can, imagine that the graves will open and these resurrected bodies will once again join their souls. So, for the first time, these souls will be "clothed" with their resurrected bodies. The Lord will descend with a shout, "Get up! You've been dead long enough!" and the bodies will appear.

Jesus taught that the day is coming when the dead shall hear His voice, and they shall be resurrected, some to the resurrection of life and some to the resurrection of damnation (John 5:28–29). Although, as we shall explain later, these resurrections take place at different times, be assured that in the end, everyone must respond to the voice of Jesus. When He shouts, the dead hear His voice and come out of their graves.

Notice that Paul refers to "the voice of an archangel" (v. 16). This is probably a reference to Gabriel. I'm of the opinion that many angels will accompany this event. They were there when Jesus was born. They were on hand at His ascension and will likewise accompany Him when He returns. At the second stage of His coming, known as the glorious appearing, they are explicitly mentioned as being present (2 Thessalonians 1:7–8).

Then we read that there will be the sound of "the trumpet call of God" (v. 16). What was the trumpet used for in Old Testament times? Blowing the trumpet signified that it was time to pack up and move. When Israel camped in the wilderness for forty years and it was time to break camp, a trumpet would be blown. You can imagine that the entire camp of Israelites began to stir and even those who were asleep in their tents would be roused from sleep and begin to move to their next destination. So, Jesus will come with a blast of a trumpet, and the dead in Christ will rise because the time to move up to heaven will have come.

THE LIVING ARE INSTANTLY TRANSFORMED

What about those who are alive when the rapture takes place? The dead in Christ rise first; "After that, we who are still alive and are left will be caught up together with them in the clouds" (v. 17). So, those who are alive when the rapture happens actually are transformed *after* the dead in Christ rise. The dead have a very brief time advantage (perhaps because they have a bit farther to go!).

ABRAHAM, MOSES, AND DAVID, AND A HOST OF OTHERS DIED AS BELIEVERS BUT THEY DID NOT DIE "IN CHRIST."

I believe that this expression "the dead in Christ" refers only to all who have believed in Christ since the formation of the church on the day of Pentecost. The body of Christ was formed on that special day and so the "dead in Christ" does not include Old Testament saints. Abraham, Moses, and David, and a host of others died as believers but they did not die "in Christ." The redeemed of the Old Testament will be raised at the second stage of the coming of Christ, at His glorious appearing (to be discussed later). Making a proper distinction between the church and Israel is a further reason to believe in the pretribulation rapture which sees the return of Christ as two stages, not just one.

At the rapture, the scene will be reminiscent of the resurrection of Lazarus. Jesus was at the tomb of a dead man (John 11). It was when Jesus spoke the words, "Lazarus, come out!" (v. 43) that his soul reconnected with his body and he returned to life. The church father Augustine once noted, "We can be thankful that Jesus said, 'Lazarus come forth.' If he hadn't named him, the whole cemetery would have arisen up from the dead!" The resurrection of Lazarus was a selective resurrection, just like the resurrection of the "dead in Christ." Eventually, all the dead will be raised, but they are not raised at the same time.

So, in answer to the believers who were worried about whether their dead loved ones would be disadvantaged at the return of Christ, Paul politely tells them that they are wrong; in point of fact, the dead have a slight advantage over the living. The dead are the first to be raised and the living are then transformed so that *together* we will all go in procession to meet King Jesus. "After that, we who are still alive and are left will be caught up together [raptured] with them in the clouds to meet the Lord in the air. And so we will be with the Lord forever" (v. 17).

Paul taught that there would be an entire generation of Christians who would be alive at the return of Jesus. The same event is spoken of in 1 Corinthians 15:51–52: "Listen, I tell you a mystery: We will not all sleep, but we will all be changed—in a flash, in the twinkling of an eye, at the last trumpet. For the trumpet will sound, the dead will be raised imperishable, and we will be changed." When he says we shall not all sleep, he once again is referring to death; not all Christians will die, but will be instantly translated into heaven when the rapture happens.

We will be changed in the "twinkling of an eye." How long does it take for your eye to twinkle? I've been told that it is approximately one-fiftieth of a second! There will be an entire generation of believers who will be changed from this existence to their eternal bodies immediately; but in the seconds that precede this event, the dead in Christ will have already been raised just as quickly.

What about the expression the last trumpet"? When Jesus spoke about His glorious appearing, He also mentioned a "trumpet call." To quote Him, "And he will send his angels with a loud trumpet call, and they will gather his elect from the four winds, from one end of the heavens to the other" (Matthew 24:31). Since there will be a trumpet call at the glorious appearing and since the church is raptured at "the *last* trumpet call, posttribulationists say the rapture and the glorious return must happen simultaneously. However, I believe that the "last trumpet" should not be interpreted to mean that this is the last trumpet call to be heard, but rather it is the last trumpet for the church; it signals the end of the church age. There are other "trumpet calls" to follow, such as the trumpet judgments in the book of Revelation.

If you wish to better understand the reasons for pretribulationism, compare Paul's discussion of the rapture with the teaching about the glorious return of Christ to earth. Read Zechariah 14:1–4; Matthew 24:15–35; 2 Thessalonians 1:5–10, and Revelation 19:11–22, and then take the time to compare these passages with Paul's discussion of the rapture as described in 1 Thessalonians 4:13–18. I think it will be clear that there are two comings of Jesus, and the rapture is a very different event than the glorious return.

Consider (1) we are raptured to "meet the Lord in the air," whereas at the glorious return Jesus descends to earth, specifically to the Mount of Olives; (2) at the rapture there is no mention of Jesus fighting a battle; at the glorious return He fights to defend Jerusalem and destroys the armies who oppose His rule;

(3) the tribulation is a time when the wrath of God is poured out onto the earth, but believers are assured they are saved "from the wrath to come" (1 Thessalonians 1:10 ESV); and finally, (4) although there are no specific signs given as to when the rapture might occur, there are many signs given that anticipate the Lord's returning in power and great glory. Clearly Paul taught the believers in Thessalonica that the rapture could happen at any moment.

THE PROCESSION TO MEET KING JESUS

So, both groups, the dead in Christ and the living, will be transformed to be caught up together with Christ, in the clouds (1 Thessalonians 4:17). The appearing of Jesus is always associated with clouds; these clouds could represent either angels or human beings. The Bible says that we are presently living with a "cloud of witnesses," a reference to believers who have died (Hebrews 12:1). The clouds that accompany Jesus could also be a reference to clouds of angels or even natural clouds that accompany Jesus in His descent to earth. He ascended from the Mount of Olives and disappeared among the clouds, and He will return with clouds.

> WE WILL SING, "HAIL, KING JESUS. THANK YOU FOR COMING FOR US."

We read that we shall "meet the Lord in the air. And so we will be with the Lord forever" (v. 17). The word *meet* often was used for a delegation meeting an important person. For example, it is used of a delegation coming out to meet Paul when he arrived in Rome (Acts 28:15). It is almost as if we should visualize both the living believers who were raptured, as well as those who had previously died, now rising in their glorified bodies to meet King Jesus in glorious procession. We will sing, "Hail, King Jesus. Thank You for coming for us. Thank You for redeeming us. Here we are, Jesus, Everlasting King!"

To conclude his instruction on this topic, Paul included the phrase, "And so we will be with the Lord forever." Think about it. We are going to be with the Lord for all eternity. If pretribulationism is correct, and I believe it is, we're going to be with the Lord in heaven during the great tribulation on earth. The contrast between the suffering on earth and the bliss of heaven at this point is beyond our imagination.

It's not just that we will be with Jesus, glorious though that is. But it is also about being there with the whole family of God and our loved ones. That's why the apostle Paul ends by commanding, "Therefore encourage each other with these words" (v. 18). When someone dies as a believer and we say we will see them again, we really mean it. The departures on earth for Christians are never permanent. We never really say goodbye. We only say, "See you soon."

Earlier in this passage, Paul speaks of those who have died as those who "fall asleep" (v. 13). The imagery of "sleeping in Jesus" is one that intimately connects with a mother and a child. After a mother feeds a newborn baby, she will rock the baby gently to sleep. When a Christian dies, it is as if Jesus has lulled him/her to sleep in His arms, and then later the child will rise to be with Him forever and ever. So, we do not "grieve like the rest of men, who have no hope" (v. 13).

Cyprian, a writer from the third century, observed that if it were not for the plagues, Christianity would have never swept North Africa. Why? He said that during the plagues, Christians were filled with anticipation of seeing Christ and the pagans died without hope. The pagans said of the Christians, "They carry their dead as if in triumph. Where is all this hope coming from?" Early Christians bore witness to the saving grace of Jesus, because Christians died differently. The Lord is going to return from heaven and the believers will be snatched away, and the dead in Christ will rise.

WHAT THIS MEANS FOR US

The implications for us are momentous, aren't they?

First, we should be looking for the return of Christ. We need not be looking for the rise of Antichrist and other signs that will eventually be revealed as the great tribulation is about to begin. Of course, as we shall point out, we may even in our day see certain geopolitical events take shape that make us think we are nearing the time when God wraps up history, but that should not be our focus. A bride in waiting yearns to be married to her Beloved.

Paul said that a special reward was given to him and to all those who long for the Lord's appearing (2 Timothy 4:8). This anticipation should motivate us to holy living. Listen to what the apostle John says: "Dear friends, now we are children of God, and what we will be has not yet been made known. But we know that when he appears, we shall be like him, for we shall see him as he is" (1 John 3:2).

THE RETURN OF CHRIST IS PRESENTED TO CHANGE US, TO REORDER OUR PRIORITIES.

We will be like Christ; we will have a body like that of Jesus. There will be no cancer, no aches, no pains, no need for sleep, and no aging. We will be like Him "for we shall see him as he is."

It is clear that the New Testament doesn't give us these prophetic words just to satisfy our curiosity. To quote John again: "Everyone who has this hope in him purifies himself, just as he is pure" (1 John 3:3). The return of Christ is presented to change us, to reorder our priorities. It is a motivation to holiness. Evangelist D. L. Moody's favorite verse was, "The world and its desires pass away, but the man who does the will of God lives forever" (1 John 2:17).

Second, it's a motivation for us to be busy serving the Lord, doing those things that please Him. As we shall learn in the next chapter, we as believers will give an account for the way in which we lived. Whether we will be rewarded or "lose our rewards" is determined by our lifestyle, our priorities and motives.

Sometimes we can learn lessons from the animal kingdom. Indeed, the Lord laments, "The ox knows his master, the donkey his owner's manger, but Israel does not know, my people do not understand" (Isaiah 1:3). As you know, dogs are very loyal. There is a story about a farmer who had a very close relationship with his dog, and when the old man died they took his body, put it in a coffin, and put it on the train. According to the story that I was told, this dog ran toward the train every single day when it came to the station. The dog was always hoping that the train that took his master away would eventually bring him back. We as God's children should live each day with the same anticipation.

YOU CAN LOVE JESUS FOR THE WRONG REASONS.

At the Parliament of World Religions held in Chicago many years ago, I met a woman from another religion. I asked her if she loved Jesus. She said, "Oh yes, I love Him," and she began to cry. I said, "Why?" She answered, "I love Him because of all the miracles He did. I love Him because He loved children. I love Him, I love Him, I love Him." Then I looked directly into her eyes and asked, "Do you also love Him because He died on the cross as a sacrifice for our sins so that we could be forgiven and know God?" She broke eye contact with me and said, "I never thought of that before."

Yes, you can even love Jesus for the wrong reasons. What a tragedy to know Shakespeare but not as a man of literature; to know Newton but not as a scientist; to know Jesus but not as a Savior and King. I urge you today, if you've never settled the issue of making Jesus your Savior, do not read another chapter without realizing that He died on the cross for our sins and was raised so that we could know Him, and so that we could be reconciled to

God, and so that we could be "in Christ."

Like a magnet that attracts only iron filings, so the first coming of Jesus will draw only those who know Him into the clouds to meet Him in the air. As this book progresses, we will learn what happens to those who are left behind. The difference between the "two eternities" is beyond the human imagination.

Face to face with Christ, my Savior,
Face to face—what will it be,
When with rapture I behold Him,
Jesus Christ who died for me?
—Carrie E. Breck

CHAPTER TWO

THE KING
JUDGES US

*Fix your eyes on your heavenly reward
instead of earthly allurements.*
—Charles Swindoll

Imagine, tears in heaven!

We read, "He will wipe every tear from their eyes" (Revelation 21:4). The question we are forced to ask ourselves is: Why are there tears in heaven? Why would God need to wipe away them away? Two answers have been suggested: one is that we will be grieved because some people we love will not be in heaven; we can imagine a mother whose son does not appear in heaven's roll count. Well might she cry.

But there is a second reason why there might be tears in heaven, and perhaps it is correct: we will weep when we are awash with regret for the selfish lives we lived on earth. We may very well weep because of how badly we fare as we stand before the Lord at the judgment seat of Jesus Christ.

The judgment seat of Christ is the judgment at which all Christians will appear. This judgment is to be distinguished from the judgment of the great white throne which will be discussed in detail in chapter 9 of this book. At the great white throne judgment, all unbelievers will give an account to God. It is terrifying in its scope and implications.

WE MAY VERY WELL WEEP BECAUSE OF HOW BADLY WE FARE AS WE STAND BEFORE THE LORD.

However, I believe that this judgment is the one where all of us as believers will be called into account and it will take place after the rapture of the church. Attendance is compulsory; no excuses, no continuances, no attorney to put the best spin on our lives. We read, "So we make it our goal to please him, whether we are at home in the body or away from it. For we must all appear before the judgment seat of Christ, that each one may receive what is due him for the things done while in the body, whether good or bad" (2 Corinthians 5:9–10).

HOW TO THINK ABOUT THE JUDGMENT SEAT

There are several misconceptions about this event. Some Christians think, "Well, since it doesn't determine whether or not I am going to heaven and only has to do with rewards, the way in which I live now isn't really that important. After all, doesn't 'Calvary cover it all'?"

First, let me be clear that "Calvary *does* cover it all" as the hymn reminds us. When we receive Jesus Christ as Savior, our sins are forgiven legally—past, present, and future—but this doesn't mean we can live as we wish. God disciplines us when we become disobedient, and He judges sin wherever it is found. In Acts 5 we find the story of Ananias and Sapphira. They told a lie to the apostle Peter, and as a result God judged them with death. I can imagine that when they arrived in heaven, they might have said, "What is this? We are believers and thought that Calvary covered it all." Well, yes, if they were believers, they were legally forgiven for their sins and their place in heaven was assured. But we need to distinguish our arrival in heaven from God's discipline and assessment of how we served Him. At the judgment seat, the disobedient Christian will not receive the same rewards as a Christian who spent his life selflessly in the service of Christ. Today is preparation for tomorrow.

Another misconception is that it is selfish to talk about "earning rewards" as a proper motivation for faithfully serving the Lord. Some say, "Why should I care about eternal rewards? Isn't being in heaven with Jesus enough?" Or perhaps you've heard it said, "Isn't it true that these rewards are crowns that we will just cast at the feet of Jesus anyway?"

THESE REWARDS ARE POSITIONS OF RESPONSIBILITY IN THE COMING KINGDOM.

We may receive crowns that we will cast at Jesus' feet, but if we do so, we're going to pick them up again because we will rule with Christ forever. Keep in mind that these rewards are positions of responsibility in the coming kingdom. If you are faithful with little, you will rule over much. If you are unfaithful with little, you will be denied ruling over that which is much (see Matthew 25:21).

One day a man told me, "I am a Christian but I'm backslidden. I'm just doing my own thing. When I get to heaven, as long as I get a backseat somewhere I will be happy." I answered him, "That sounds so humble. But what if Jesus intended you be in the front row, to use your analogy, but the reason you are in a backseat is because you displeased Him?" One Christian said to me, "I'll be satisfied if I just have a little shack in heaven!" Interestingly, however, I observed that he was by no means satisfied with a little shack on earth. Our excuses for not living heartily for Christ simply do not wash.

The apostle Paul connects pleasing Christ with how well we will do at the judgment seat. (Reread 2 Corinthians 5:9–10, quoted above.) Imagine the regret of a Christian who is in the "in the back row," so to speak, because he didn't please Christ. To seek rewards is not selfish—in fact, Jesus frequently motivated His disciples with the promise of rewards. We should all hope to do well at this judgment because that will prove we have pleased Christ.

Puritan theologian Jonathan Edwards said that he would use all the energy he had to gain as many rewards as possible, because the more rewards he got, the more pleasing he would be to Christ. So, excuses aside, God's challenge to us today is: *go for rewards.*

OUR WORKS TORCHED WITH FIRE

The first and perhaps most familiar passage on rewards is 1 Corinthians 3:10–15. Even if we are well acquainted with it, we do well to read it carefully again. Paul writes:

> By the grace God has given me, I laid a foundation as an expert builder, and someone else is building on it. But each one should be careful how he builds. For no one can lay any foundation other than the one already laid, which is Jesus Christ. If any man builds on this foundation using gold, silver, costly stones, wood, hay or straw, his work will be shown for what it is, because the Day will bring it to light. It will be revealed with fire, and the fire will test the quality of each man's work. If what he has built survives, he will receive his reward. If it is burned up, he will suffer loss; he himself will be saved, but only as one escaping through the flames.

Paul says that we should think of our lives and our ministries either as gold, silver, or precious stones; or as wood, hay, and stubble. When God torches our works, the truth will come out as to what kind of people we really were and whom we really served here on earth.

Many years ago, after a wildfire in Colorado, my wife, Rebecca, and I drove past some of the destroyed homes. It was unbelievable. There was nothing left of the beautiful houses except the chimneys and charred foundations. Everything combustible was gone; only what was made of brick and concrete survived. Why? In the very same way, the apostle Paul says there are some believers who will make it to heaven, but their works will be burned up; but yet they will be saved—even though only as one escaping through the flames (v. 15).

Dr. Harry Ironside, who occupied the pulpit of Moody Church during the 1940s, said there are some people who will make it to heaven but will smell as if they were bought in a fire sale! The imagery is that as they enter heaven their lives will collapse behind them. Everything will go up in smoke. What a tragedy. Sobering.

THREE WAYS WE WILL BE JUDGED

Let's repeat the key verse regarding the judgment seat of Christ. "So we make it our goal to please him, whether we are at home in the body or away from it. For we must all appear before the judgment seat of Christ, that each one may receive what is due him for the things done while in the body, whether good or bad" (2 Corinthians 5:9–10). As we investigate this topic let me share three characteristics of the judgment seat of Christ, and then I will explain why anticipating this event should change our lives.

JESUS DESIRES FOR US TO DO WELL AS WE STAND BEFORE HIM.

WE WILL BE JUDGED FAIRLY

Remember, this is the judgment seat *of Jesus Christ*. He who died to redeem us now lives to judge us. Jesus desires for us to do well as we stand before Him. Because He knows all things, He will take all of the contingencies into account. He will take a careful look at your life: how you were impacted by your parents, and the positive or negative effect that others had on you, and every other relevant factor as you stand before Him. His evaluation will be accurate and perfect and fair.

You may be thinking, "Will I be given the opportunity to defend myself?" I suspect if you care to you can, but I even more strongly suspect that we will see the foolishness of such a move. Imagine the piercing eyes of Jesus staring at us; trust me, you and I will be absolutely convinced that what Jesus sees and says will be right and true. His meticulous justice will overwhelm us. There will be no way to tweak our record. We will be in the presence of nothing but reality.

We will be judged from the point in time when we received Jesus Christ as Savior—till the time of our death. I don't believe that we will be judged for the way we lived in our preconversion days. The apostle Paul expected to do well, even though he was doing terrible things before his conversion. He persecuted the early church, gave approval to the death of Stephen, and was on his way to Damascus to arrest Christians when Jesus revealed Himself along the way. Yet despite Paul's past, he could write, "I have fought the good fight, I have finished the race, I have kept the faith. Now there is in store for me the crown of righteousness, which the Lord, the righteous Judge, will award to me on that day—and not only to me, but also to all who have longed for his appearing" (2 Timothy 4:7–8). Paul knew his rewards would be solely based on what he had accomplished since his dramatic conversion on the road to Damascus.

A woman asked me, "Do I still have any opportunity to do well at the judgment seat? In my preconversion days I was involved in some pornographic films, and even now they are still being played and so their evil influence continues." I responded, "Dear sister, yes, if you are faithful with what God has now given you, living a life that glorifies Him, you too can do well at the judgment seat of Jesus Christ." We will be judged fairly.

WE WILL BE JUDGED INDIVIDUALLY

The second characteristic is much more personal: *we will be judged individually.* Paul says we must appear before the judgment seat so that *"each one* may receive what is due him for the things done while in the body, whether good or bad" (v. 10, italics added). Every Christian will individually experience this judgment seat; we will be individually reviewed.

In Romans, Paul makes this point even clearer: "You, then, why do you judge your brother? Or why do you look down on your brother? For we will all stand before God's judgment seat. . . . So then, *each of us will give an account of himself to God"* (14:10, 12; italics added). To restate this concept in contemporary terms, let's suppose you are critical of some of your Christian friends. Paul is saying, in effect, "Don't you dare judge them. They will individually give an account to God and so will you. They may actually do better than you at the judgment seat of Christ."

WHEN YOU AND I ARE FACE-TO-FACE WITH JESUS, THE ONLY THING THAT WILL MATTER IS THE EXPRESSION ON HIS FACE.

I attended a Bible college in Canada that was so small that the entire student body of about sixty sang in the choir. The only requirement to sing in the choir was to be enrolled in this Bible college. I am not a terrible singer, but there were some songs that were a little difficult or I didn't know the words, so I just mouthed them because I knew that everybody else would cover for me. No one knew the difference.

But when you and I stand before Jesus, we will all have to

sing a solo with no accompaniment! There will be no one to hide behind to make us look good. There will be no favorable comparison with the person standing next to us. No attorney to present our case or offer plausible excuses. Just us individually, standing before Jesus who knows everything.

Is this judgment going to be public? We all hope not. Some people visualize that it will be in a large stadium with everyone watching. And there are some parables Jesus told that indicate our judgment might be public. You may remember Jesus said, "So take the talent from him and give it to him who has the ten talents" (Matthew 25:28 ESV). But God is not out to shame us in the presence of our friends.

But if this judgment is public, please keep two things in mind. First, we'll all be in the same predicament; and second, I don't think it will matter whether we are in the presence of others or not. When you and I are face-to-face with Jesus, the only thing that will matter is the expression on His face. Our eyes and ears will be entirely focused on Him, wondering whether or not we will hear "Well done, good and faithful servant!"

Yes, this will be a personal judgment. We as Christians will not be compared with any other person. We will be one-on-one with Jesus, each one of us giving an account of ourselves to God. You won't be expected to account for your wife or husband. It will be your record alone that will be examined.

WE WILL BE JUDGED THOROUGHLY

Several descriptions of this judgment assure us that we will be judged *thoroughly*. We've already read, "For we must all *appear* before the judgment seat of Christ" (2 Corinthians 5:10, italics added). The Greek word for "appear" is a word that means "to be revealed"; yes, we will be revealed before the judgment seat of Jesus Christ. One commentator says that it means "to be laid bare."

As children we might say to one another, "You have some money in your pocket," and the reply would be, "No, I don't." Then whoever was asking the question would say, "Yes, you do. I don't believe you." Then the other child would turn his pocket inside out and would reveal every piece of lint to prove his point. This same imagery was already referred to in 1 Corinthians 3:13 (KJV) where Paul says that our works "shall be made manifest: for the day shall declare it, because it shall be revealed by fire." In summary, we have three words or phrases used to describe this judgment. Our works will be "made manifest," they will be "revealed by fire," and we will give an account "for the deeds done while in the body, whether good or bad" (2 Corinthians 5:10).

> THE JUDGMENT SEAT IS THE PLACE OF EVALUATION; IT IS NOT THE PLACE OF PUNISHMENT.

Stop to consider what Paul wrote elsewhere: "Therefore judge nothing before the appointed time; wait till the Lord comes. He will bring to light what is hidden in darkness and will expose the motives of men's hearts" (1 Corinthians 4:5). Can you get any more thorough than that?

John Murray, a respected theologian, said that at the judgment seat of Christ Christians will desire this judgment to finally see the depths of God's grace in saving them and then put the sins and failures of the past behind them forever. Let me share an example. Let's say a married Christian man leaves his wife and runs off with the woman of his dreams. He abandons his wife and children and marries his true love and goes to live elsewhere. He neglects his former wife and the children that he has left behind. The pain he inflicted on his wife and children is immeasurable, and they pass this legacy on to their children. He dies and goes to heaven, and there he meets his ex-wife and children. What do you think Jesus is going to do? Will He say, "Well now, let's just let bygones be bygones. The two of you just hold hands and walk into eternity and pretend that your sins on earth just don't matter"? Not for a moment do I believe that is going to be the response of Jesus. The judgment seat of Christ is the place where all such issues still need resolution.

When Paul wrote that we should not avenge ourselves (Romans 12:19) this also applies to relationships between believers. The reason we don't have to avenge ourselves in our personal relationships, even with other Christians, is because at the judgment seat of Christ, Jesus will set the record straight. That's why it's so important for us as believers to resolve as many conflicts as possible while we are on earth so that there will be fewer issues to adjudicate when we reach heaven.

Question: Are we going to see our sins at the judgment seat? Aren't they all "cast into the depths of the sea" (Micah 7:19 ESV)? If we do see our sins, we will certainly see them as having been forgiven, because our sins will no longer be held against us. The judgment seat is the place of evaluation and resolution; it is not the place of punishment, for Jesus bore our punishment on the cross. "Therefore, there is now no condemnation for those who are in Christ Jesus" (Romans 8:1).

What if—and I'm speculating here—what if Jesus took all of our works and translated them either into gold, silver, and precious stones; or wood, hay, and stubble. Then He would torch the pile as it is laid before Him. This would provide a powerful evaluation of your life and mine without us having to see any of our sins. The point, of course, is that it is a thorough judgment, even though our sins are legally taken away.

HE WILL FIND SOMETHING GOOD IN ALL OF US FOR WHICH TO PRAISE US.

Might Jesus be angry with us? No, all the anger of God was appeased when Jesus Christ died on the cross. Yet I can't help but think that He might be disappointed in the way in which we have lived in light of His many blessings toward us. Paul says we should live in such a way that we "please him," which means that we can also live in such a way that displeases Him. Be assured He loves us no matter how well or poorly we do. And finally, here is this word of encouragement: He will find something good in all of us for which to praise us: "At that time each will receive his praise from God" (1 Corinthians 4:5).

There is a man who had a dream in which all of his life was piled in one big heap represented by various materials that he could not identify. Then Jesus took a match and lit the pile, and it burned brightly. When the smoke died down, before him was a heap of ashes. He took a small brush and brushed those ashes away. But as he did this, he noticed small nuggets of gold, little bits of silver, and a few precious stones. He took these precious metals and brushed them into a little tin. Of course, it was only a dream, but maybe it is a rather accurate picture of what our judgment will be like.

Let's not take the word *judgment* out of the phrase, "the judgment seat of Christ." We have a serious appointment with Jesus. And, thankfully, we still have time to prepare for it!

WHAT JESUS WILL BE LOOKING FOR

What will Jesus be looking for? What in His opinion will survive the fire? Without question that is one of the most important questions we could ever ask.

First, He will seek for our joyous acceptance of injustice and false accusations. "Blessed are you when people insult you, persecute you and falsely say all kinds of evil against you because of me. Rejoice and be glad, because great is your reward in heaven, for in the same way they persecuted the prophets who were before you" (Matthew 5:11–12).) As believers, we are expected to endure hardship and persecution. And while suffering for Christ

IT WAS BILLY GRAHAM WHO SAID, "IF A PERSON GETS HIS ATTITUDE TOWARD MONEY STRAIGHT, IT WILL HELP STRAIGHTEN OUT ALMOST EVERY OTHER AREA IN HIS LIFE."

has been the experience of the church throughout history, it is intensifying even in the United States. In the last few years at least seven books have been written saying that Christians are the real jihad, and that Christians are the ones that Americans should really fear. False evidence and false accusations will increasingly be used against us. If we respond to such accusations with joy, such an attitude will survive the fire of the judgment.

Second, Jesus will evaluate our financial generosity. "Do not store up for yourselves treasures on earth, where moths and vermin destroy, and where thieves break in and steal. But store up for yourselves treasures in heaven, where moths and vermin do not destroy, and where thieves do not break in and steal. For where your treasure is, there your heart will be also" (Matthew 6:19–21). Stingy Christians should question whether they are Christians at all. Christians are expected to be generous, giving, and eager to help. It was Billy Graham who said, "If a person gets his attitude toward money straight, it will help straighten out almost every other area in his life."[1]

Third, Jesus will reveal the extent of our hospitality. Read this remarkable commentary:

> When you give a luncheon or dinner, do not invite your friends, your brothers or relatives, or your rich neighbors; if you do, they may invite you back and so you will be repaid. But when you give a banquet, invite the poor, the crippled, the lame, the blind, and you will be blessed. Although they cannot repay you, you will be repaid at the resurrection of the righteous. (Luke 14:12–14)

Unfortunately, many of us, content as introverts, have the philosophy that we should "leave others alone and be left alone."

This may be the mind-set of our culture, but it should not be our attitude. We are called to show hospitality, to care for the lonely, to reach out to our neighbors. In fact, the reason Christianity spread during the early centuries is because the Christians practiced generous hospitality. John Piper writes, "If you are afraid of hospitality—that you don't have much personal strength or personal wealth—good. Then you won't intimidate anybody. You will depend all the more on God's grace. You will look all the more to the work of Christ and not your own work. And what a blessing people will get in your simple home or little apartment."[2]

JESUS WILL REVEAL TO US THE EXTENT TO WHICH WE LOVED THE UNLOVABLE.

Fourth, Jesus will review our faithfulness in our vocation. Paul wrote, "And whatever you do, whether in word or deed, do it all in the name of the Lord Jesus, giving thanks to God the Father through him" (Colossians 3:17). Want to be rewarded by Jesus? Do your job *for* Jesus; go to work because you are serving Him, not your boss or the company. A joyful attitude, heartily working despite unfairness, merits reward at the judgment seat.

Fifth, Jesus will reveal to us the extent to which we loved the unlovable. "But love your enemies, do good to them, and lend to them without expecting to get anything back. Then your reward will be great, and you will be sons of the Most High, because he is kind to the ungrateful and wicked" (Luke 6:35). Perhaps God will bring someone into your life who is difficult to love. Why? To paraphrase, God says, "I bring them into your life because I want you to have many rewards. Start loving them and your reward will be great" (see Luke 6:32–36).

Do you realize how faithful Jesus is? A cup of water given in His name and you will not lose your reward (Matthew 10:42). Our good works are an expression of our devotion to Jesus as His children. Although all of our works are still tainted with sin,

Jesus takes them and cleanses them so that they are acceptable to the Father. The Bible says that we are to "offer spiritual sacrifices acceptable to God through Jesus Christ" (1 Peter 2:5 ESV). Yes, even when we do those works that merit reward, it will be because they have been made acceptable to God by Jesus Christ.

Incredibly, Jesus gives us the desire and strength to do good works and then rewards us for the works He gives us the grace to do! From beginning to end, it is all a gift of disproportionate and undeserved grace. If we love Him, it is only because He first loved us!

TRANSFORMING LESSONS

Let me share some lessons with you that have had an impact in my own life. First, it's very clear that every day we live is either a plus or a minus so far as our rewards are concerned. Either we contribute to our precious metal collection or we add to our pile of wood, hay, and stubble. Our lives, of course, are a mixture of both.

I was watching an interview Diane Sawyer had with evangelist Billy Graham. She said to Billy, "How would you like to be remembered?" He responded, "I'd like to hear 'Well done, thou good and faithful servant,' but I don't think I will." Immediately two thoughts came to my mind: "Billy Graham is being more humble than he needs to be!" And second, I thought, "If Billy Graham was not sure if he was going to do well at the judgment seat, what about the rest of us?"

But what Billy Graham said was true from this standpoint: He's not going to hear "Well done" because he preached to large crowds. That was his calling. The real question is not going to be how large the crowds were or the number of people who accepted Christ as Savior as a result of his efforts. The real question will be, "Billy, were you faithful with what I gave you?" That's why we can say with truthfulness that the people who will be rewarded the greatest are not necessarily the people who are well known. The best reward might go to the car dealer who ran an honest business; the prize will go to the missionary who served in obscurity but was faithful with what God gave him or her to do. Those are the ones who will really be rewarded. But every moment is either a loss or a gain as far as rewards are concerned.

One day a man whose wife had a debilitating disease drove me to the airport. He told me how the disease affected his wife and she repeatedly became very irritable, very critical, and impossible to please. The stories he told about his life with her made me wonder how he kept his sanity. When we said goodbye I said to him, half-joking, "I don't expect to see you in heaven." He was a little surprised, but then I said, "No, I really don't expect to see you there. I think you are going to be so close to the front of the line, and I'm going to be so far back that we'll probably never meet!" Though I shared the words with humor, I have no doubt his reward will be great—much greater than mine.

> THE POSSIBILITY OF RECEIVING THE APPROVAL OF CHRIST SHOULD MAKE US THROW CAUTION TO THE WINDS AND LIVE PASSIONATELY FOR HIS GLORY ALONE.

So the people who will be the most rewarded will not necessarily be those with the largest churches or best-selling books. The most honored will be those who are faithful in their calling, whatever it may be. As missionary C. T. Studd was known for saying, "Only one life will soon be past, only what's done for Christ will last."

Second, the possibility of receiving the approval of Christ should make us throw caution to the winds and live passionately for His glory alone during the few days we have left here on earth. Just to think, if we are faithful we will get to rule with Him. Perhaps in the end all Christians will reign with Christ, but it is interesting that in the New Testament a connection is often made between reigning with Christ and faithfulness. For example, Paul wrote, "If we have died with him, we will also live with him; if we endure, we will also reign with him" (2 Timothy 2:11–12). Or consider these words in Revelation 3:21: "To him who overcomes, I will give the right to sit with me on my throne, just as I overcame and sat down with my Father on his throne." Now there's one sense in which all Christians are overcomers because they have believed in Jesus Christ as Savior, but I cannot believe that somebody who has squandered his life with selfish living will receive the same reward as the Christian who lived his life faithfully.

Will everyone in heaven be happy? Yes, everyone will joyfully be serving Christ. Just like a chandelier that has bulbs of different intensities, yet all give light to the room, just so everyone in heaven will be contributing to the glory of God. But not all will burn equally bright, if I might speak of it that way. But if we are faithful, just imagine hearing from Jesus, "Well done, good and faithful servant . . . Enter into the joy of [my Lord!]" (Matthew 25:21 ESV).

What is it that we can lose? Although some Bible teachers disagree with me, I believe that not everyone will hear "Well done." Jesus told several parables about faithfulness, some servants receiving commendation from their master and others receiving strong rebuke (see Matthew 25:24–30; Luke 19:20–27). We shouldn't take Christ's approval for granted.

In India there's a story often told about a wealthy rajah, a prince. He was traveling in his expensive chariot when a beggar came and stood at the side of the road. The beggar had a bowl of rice and held it out, hoping the rajah would stop to give him something. To the beggar's surprise and delight, the rajah stepped down from his chariot and said, "Beggar, give me some of your rice." The beggar was angry. *Who was this man to ask me for some of my rice?* But gingerly he took one grain of rice and gave it to the wealthy man. The rajah was unsatisfied. "Beggar, give me *more* of your rice." By now the beggar was furious, but he took another grain of rice and handed it over to the rajah. Again the rajah insisted, "Beggar, give me even *more* of your rice." By now the beggar was in a fury. He took one more grain of rice and handed it to the rajah who then returned to his chariot and rode off.

In his anger, the beggar looked into his bowl and noticed something glittering. It was a grain of gold the size of a grain of rice. He looked more carefully and found just two more grains of gold—one for each of the grains of rice he had given to the prince.

When we come to Jesus, He exchanges our rice for His gold, and it's the kind of gold that will survive the fire. What are we withholding from Jesus? What are we hanging on to, saying, "This belongs to me and not to Jesus"? When eternity comes we shall all appear before the judgment seat of Christ to give an account for the deeds done in the body whether good or bad.

Let us live in such a way as to hear, "Well done, my good and faithful servant."

NOTES

1. Billy Graham, as cited at http://christian-quotes.ochristian.com/christian-quotes_ochristian.cgi?query=money&action=Search&x=0&y=0.

2. John Piper, as cited at http://christian-quotes.ochristian.com/christian-quotes_ochristian.cgi?query=hospitality&action=Search&x=0&y=0.

CHAPTER THREE

THE KING
MARRIES HIS BRIDE

Whether we live till Christ comes again, or whether we
fall asleep in Him, many of us know that we shall sit down at
the great wedding feast in the end of the days and we shall partake
of the supper of the Lamb in the day of His joy and Glory!
. . . [It] will be the bringing of the people of God into the closest
and happiest union with Christ their Lord in Glory.
—Charles Haddon Spurgeon

A wedding like no other.

Take a moment to think about the most blessed wedding you have ever attended. (If you are married, I hope your own wedding is the first to come to mind!) This chapter is about a more spectacular marriage in heaven—a wedding ceremony— and banquet that is very literally "out of this world." There are no vows that say "until death do us part" because the marriage covenant has already been ratified and there is no death that will ever part the bridegroom and his bride. It is the marriage supper attended by King Jesus, His church. and other invited guests.

The description given in the Bible is beyond comprehension. Yet we should seek to understand this future event, to try to visualize it and contemplate its meaning. If we grasp its significance our lives will be changed forever. Imagine attending a heavenly wedding feast to celebrate our own marriage to King Jesus!

The description of the marriage supper is found in Revelation 19. The rapture and the judgment seat of Christ have already taken place. Jesus is preparing for the second stage of His coming—His glorious appearing on the Mount of Olives when He will bring us with him. He came *for* the saints in the rapture; He will soon be coming *with* His saints in the glorious appearing. But just before second stage of His return we will enjoy the marriage supper of the Lamb.

Most books on prophecy would place this chapter later, after a discussion of the great tribulation period and therefore just before the glorious return of Christ. I have chosen to discuss this great event here for the simple reason that the festivities might begin soon after the judgment seat of Christ, and perhaps extend throughout the tribulation period on earth. Regardless of the chronology, we must give our attention to this spectacular event, especially because we as believers will be present.

LESSONS FROM JEWISH WEDDING TRADITION

Let's review the context. In Revelation 19:6 we read, "Then I heard what sounded like a great multitude, like the roar of rushing waters and like loud peals of thunder, shouting: 'Hallelujah! For our Lord God Almighty reigns.'" And after that exclamation of praise, we are introduced to the wedding feast. "Let us rejoice and be glad and give him glory! For the wedding of the Lamb has come, and his bride has made herself ready. Fine linen, bright and clean, was given her to wear" (Revelation 19:7–8).

This event is best understood in light of the Jewish wedding customs of the time. The first stage was, of course, the engagement, often arranged by the parents. The two sets of parents would meet together to decide which son and which daughter would marry. In our modern culture we say, "I have to fall in love first and then I will marry." The Jewish custom was, "Get married first and fall in love later." This engagement was so firm that it was considered equivalent to the marriage vow itself. Yes, there was an elaborate ceremony if you wanted to break the engagement, but such a breach of trust was rare.

The engagement usually lasted a year or two and gave each would-be spouse the opportunity to see whether or not his/her partner was being true to the vows that were yet to be made. Incidentally, that's why Joseph had such a problem with Mary when she became pregnant with Jesus. He was already engaged to her (or betrothed) and now suddenly she was pregnant. So it appeared as if she had violated their agreement. He was confused, not knowing how to respond. His initial plan was to divorce her quietly rather than have her face social embarrassment. An angel had to come and explain to him that Mary's pregnancy was a miracle, and Joseph was to take her as his wife (Matthew 1:18–25).

During this engagement period, the parents of the groom paid a dowry to the parents of the bride. In this way, the decision was ratified, proof that the partners were serious in their commitment to marry. Sometimes this dowry was paid to the future bride herself, but typically the money was paid to her family. And sometimes the amount was practically unaffordable.

Consider that Jesus, our Bridegroom, paid a dowry for us. He shed His blood "because you were slain, and with your blood you purchased men for God from every tribe and language and people and nation. You have made them to be a kingdom and

> JESUS IS THE ONLY GROOM WHO LAID DOWN HIS LIFE FOR HIS BRIDE AND THEN WAS RESURRECTED, THAT HE MIGHT BE ABLE TO REDEEM HER, CLEANSE HER, AND MARRY HER.

priests to serve our God, and they will reign on the earth" (Revelation 5:9–10).

Perhaps this explains why the wedding feast we will attend is not called "the marriage supper of the Creator." The reason this event is referred to as "the marriage supper of the Lamb" is that it is the Lamb who gave Himself for us. Jesus is the only groom who laid down His life for His bride and then was resurrected, that He might be able to redeem her, cleanse her, and marry her.

Following the engagement period came the second stage of the wedding festivities, namely, when the groom came to get his bride. The groom would often spend the engagement period building an addition onto the home of his father, and this extra room(s) was the place where he and his bride would later live. The groom took delight in preparing it, knowing that his bride would enjoy it with him. Pains were taken that the room(s) would be ready so that when they moved in together they would have furniture and amenities according to her standards or desires. This is the background to the words of Jesus:

> Do not let your hearts be troubled. Trust in God; trust also in me. In my Father's house are many rooms; if it were not so, I would have told you. I am going there to prepare a place for you. And if I go and prepare a place for you, I will come back and take you to be with me that you also may be where I am. (John 14:1–3)

Jesus purchased His people when He died on the cross for our sins. The dowry was paid to God the Father, and now Jesus, betrothed to us, was going away to prepare a dwelling place for millions of people who would constitute His bride. Yes, this would be a house with "many rooms." Then, His work completed,

He returns in the rapture to take His bride to Himself.

Believe me, there will be a great celebration when the bride arrives in the Father's house! And how will this bride look? As we have already noted, the bride will be a highly diverse body, with people "from every kindred, every tongue, and every nation." The different cultures and countries of the world will all be represented. Here at The Moody Church where I serve, we recently took a survey of our own congregation and discovered that our membership included people from over seventy different countries of origin. This is but a small glimpse of the diversity we will experience in eternity at the wedding supper of the Lamb!

FINALLY, THE MARRIAGE FEAST

Following the groom's return for his bride, we enter the third stage of the wedding—the marriage feast. Let's reread Revelation 19:7, "Let us rejoice and be glad and give him glory! For the wedding of the Lamb has come, and his bride has made herself ready." How did the bride make herself ready? She (that is the church) made herself ready first by trusting in Jesus Christ for her righteousness and salvation. The bride is justified by God's grace thanks to the sacrifice of Jesus on our behalf.

AS WITH ANY WEDDING, A MAJOR HIGHLIGHT IS THE ADORNMENT OF THE BRIDE.

But—and this is important—final preparations will be made at the judgment seat of Christ (discussed in the previous chapter). After the rapture, when the judgment seat is finished Jesus can finally "present her to himself as a radiant church, without stain or wrinkle or any other blemish, but holy and blameless" (Ephesians 5:27). Then and only then can it be said that all things are now ready because all the sin and failures of the bride have been accounted for. The bride now stands faultless before the throne.

As with any wedding, a major highlight is the adornment of

the bride. What will this bride be wearing? She will be clothed in fine linen, and the "fine linen stands for the righteous acts of the saints" (v. 8). We must distinguish two kinds of righteousness; as already indicated, we receive the righteousness of Jesus Christ when we receive Him as Savior, but that righteousness is worked out in our lives through our obedience. As we obey the Lord, we discover that our legal righteousness is translated into those practical works of righteousness that we have discussed in the previous chapter.

The clothes that will be worn—the linen that is white and pure and clean—represents the gold, silver, and precious stones we received at the judgment seat of Christ. Whatever survived the fire will be used to weave our garments. The good works we weave on earth we will, figuratively speaking, wear in heaven. "And if anyone gives even a cup of cold water to one of these little ones because he is my disciple, I tell you the truth, he will certainly not lose his reward" (Matthew 10:42).

Will we all be dressed in the same linen? Will we look essentially identical, dressed in the same gown or the same attire? That's one possibility, but my friend, Pastor Stephen Davey,[1] suggests that perhaps our heavenly clothing will be something like graduation garments. When you walk down the graduation aisle, your garment might be made of the same cloth as the person next to you, but some honorees wear special decorations because of their significant achievements. Perhaps—and I'm only speculating—the rewards we have received at the judgment seat will be acknowledged by the garments we wear. Everyone will be joyfully accepted, but we must never forget that the garments we will wear, the linen white and clean, will be "the righteous acts of the saints." In one way or another, our righteous deeds on earth will meet us in heaven. As

IN ONE WAY OR ANOTHER, OUR RIGHTEOUS DEEDS ON EARTH WILL MEET US IN HEAVEN.

for infants, I believe that they will appear as fully grown and not having had the opportunity to do righteous deeds, their garments will be freely granted them, for we must remember that even the garments of faithful believers are gifts of unearned grace.

THE INVITED GUESTS

In addition to the bride, there will be "invited guests." Let's continue to read the passage, "Then the angel said to me, 'Write: "Blessed are those who are invited to the wedding supper of the Lamb!" And he added, 'These are the true words of God.'" (19:9–10). Some Bible teachers think that this is a reference to the bride herself; but a bride isn't "invited" to her own wedding. To the contrary, a bride and the bridegroom invite the guests. This must be a reference to some other people who also have an invitation to the feast.

The Bible lets us speculate who these invited guests are. However, consider this: after the church is raptured and taken to heaven, there will be a period of great tribulation on the earth that lasts at least seven years and maybe longer. Daniel 12:1–3 predicts that at the end of this tribulation period there will be a resurrection, and I think that this will be when all of the Old Testament believers will be resurrected.

At that time Michael, the great prince who protects your people, will arise. There will be a time of distress such as has not happened from the beginning of nations until then. But at that time your people—everyone whose name is found written in the book—will be delivered. Multitudes who sleep in the dust of the earth will awake: some to everlasting life, others to shame and everlasting contempt. Those who are wise will shine like the brightness of the heavens, and those who lead many to righteousness, like the stars for ever and ever.

If the Old Testament saints are resurrected after the great

tribulation, they would be arriving in heaven just at the time when the marriage supper would be in progress (again we cannot know the exact sequence), but either way, they of course, would join us—the church—to descend to earth with Jesus at the glorious appearing. This interpretation is supported by Jesus, who was criticizing some of the Jewish people for thinking that they had an entitlement to the kingdom simply because they had the right lineage. Jesus rebuked them and in effect said, "You might have the right lineage physically but you don't have the right heart; you are not accepting God's Messiah."

To drive this point home, when Jesus met a centurion who had great faith, Jesus contrasted him with the self-righteous Jewish people. He said, "I say to you that many will come from the east and the west, and will take their places at the feast with Abraham, Isaac and Jacob in the kingdom of heaven. But the subjects of the kingdom will be thrown outside, into the darkness, where there will be weeping and gnashing of teeth" (Matthew 8:11–12). Notice carefully that the patriarchs—Abraham, Isaac, and Jacob—these men, representing righteous Israel, will be in the kingdom. That means that the Old Testament believers will have been resurrected before the kingdom is established. So, it would only make sense to think that they would be present in time for the marriage supper, and then all of us join together as we all return with Jesus to the Mount of Olives.

Take a moment to visualize it. Millions of people comprise the bride of Jesus Christ. And now millions more from the Old Testament era arrive to participate in the festivities. There will be Abraham, Isaac, and Jacob, and I'm sure that we will instantly recognize them. The entire list of heroes from Hebrews 11 will enter—Moses, Samson, Rahab—thousands upon thousands will gather, filing in, rank after rank as far as the eye can see. All redeemed, all washed white and clean, all free of sin, and all worshiping the bridegroom King Jesus, our Lord.

You might be wondering who will serve all of us at this feast. We might not know the complete answer to that question, but I know one person who will. This is a passage of Scripture I have often contemplated with tears in my eyes; Jesus said, "It will be good for those servants whose master finds them watching when he comes. I tell you the truth, he will dress himself to serve, will have them recline at the table and will come and wait on them" (Luke 12:37). Jesus Christ Himself will don the garments of a servant and will be our waiter! On earth, kings are served by their subjects; here at this feast, the King serves His subjects! What a rebuke to our earthly pride!

JESUS CHRIST HIMSELF WILL DON THE GARMENTS OF A SERVANT AND WILL BE OUR WAITER!

Remember when Jesus was about to wash Peter's feet, he objected. "He came to Simon Peter, who said to him, 'Lord, are you going to wash my feet?' Jesus replied, 'You do not realize now what I am doing, but later you will understand.' 'No,' said Peter, 'you shall never wash my feet.' Jesus answered, 'Unless I wash you, you have no part with me.' 'Then, Lord,' Simon Peter replied, 'not just my feet but my hands and my head as well!'" (John 13:6–9). Now in heaven, we will no longer be a victim of our own pride, but from our earthly standpoint we can imagine that we will be tempted to jump up and say, "Lord, You sit down. We're going to serve You!" And then He'll say, "Don't you remember how I taught you that in the kingdom he who serves is greater than he who rules?" This is an account that no one could possibly make up. Pause for a moment and think about it—*Jesus will ask us to remains seated as He becomes our waiter and serves us at the great feast of the kingdom!*

DRINKING WITH THE GROOM IN THE KINGDOM

What will we eat and drink? After all, a wedding feast means that food and drink will be in abundance. We don't have the menu, so we don't know the foods that will be served, but we can be quite sure what we will drink. In a Jewish wedding it was very important for the bride and the groom to drink new wine. The family would store this wine long in advance, saving it for the wedding feast. You will recall that at the wedding in Cana, Jesus turned water into wine—the best wine they'd ever tasted. The host, not knowing the source of this special wine said to the servants, "You have saved the best till now" (John 2:10).

When Jesus instituted what we call the Lord's Supper, He gathered His disciples together and in effect, said to them, "I wish to eat the Passover with you." And then when they were assembled together at a special point in the ceremony, He took bread and said, "This is my body given for you; do this in remembrance of me." Then He took the cup and said, "This cup is the new covenant in my blood, which is poured out for you" (Luke 22:19–20). Then in Matthew 26:29 Jesus made this amazing statement. He said, "I tell you, I will not drink of this fruit of the vine from now on until that day when I drink it anew with you in my Father's kingdom."

So it is. We will drink wine with Him in the Father's kingdom. The best wine—the new wine—symbolic of the blood of Christ, will be our drink in the kingdom. Together we will eat and drink; together we will have fellowship with the Bridegroom and His Father. Together we will enjoy the fellowship of "eating and drinking" in the kingdom.

Although some parts of this description of the wedding feast might be symbolic, we cannot escape the obvious point that there will be

KNOWING THAT WE ARE LOVED UNCONDITIONALLY AND PERSONALLY, WE WILL BE SPONTANEOUS IN OUR PRAISE, IN OUR OBEDIENCE AND WORSHIP.

intimacy between us and Jesus; the joy will be companionship with Him, the closeness, and the sheer freedom of being in an environment totally free from guilt, free from shame, and free from the need to compete. Knowing that we are loved unconditionally and personally, we will be spontaneous in our praise, in our obedience and worship. Heaven will, first and foremost, be about King Jesus.

I expect that although the Old Testament believers (Israel) and the New Testament believers (the church) will most likely be distinguishable in the kingdom, together we will serve the Lord with freedom and joy. If we want to spend time with Abraham, for example, we will be able to take our time, for we have all of eternity ahead of us. Even if we all spent a hundred years with each person in heaven, eternity will hardly have begun!

However, as we shall see later, in context, after the marriage supper we will return to earth with Jesus, now asserting His rightful position as King of the Earth. This return, in which we participate, can scarcely be imagined, much less grasped. And, of course this event awaits a fuller discussion in chapter 7 of this book.

Consider Paul's words, "When Christ who is your life, appears, then you also will appear with him in glory" (Colossians 3:4). Take a moment to consider what this means. When Christ returns after the marriage supper, the entire universe will see how close we are to Jesus. Every demon, every angel, every unconverted person who is on Planet Earth, will see us next to King Jesus at His appearing. We will "appear with him in glory." What more can be said?

The marriage supper of the Lamb will be very different from the weddings we now have on earth in this regard: in our weddings, all the attention is on the bride—what she's wearing, with whom she walks down the aisle. The groom just stands in front by the altar, and is hardly noticed, except when the vows begin.

But in heaven it's going to be very different. Throughout all of eternity the question will not be, "Who is the bride?" The question will be, "Who is the groom? Who is the Lamb of God that redeemed His church and cleansed her in order that He should marry her? Who is this King that descends? Who is this Alpha and Omega?" The answer, of course is that it is Jesus Christ, King of kings, Lord of lords, God of all gods. The focus will be on Him—the one who deserves unending worship.

When Dr. John Stott graduated from Cambridge, the Rev. Paul Gibson retired as principal. In honor of the man's service, a portrait of him was unveiled. In expressing thanks, Gibson paid a well-deserved compliment to the artist, saying that in the future people looking at the picture would not ask, "Who is that man?" but rather, "Who painted the portrait?"[2] Just so, throughout eternity people will not ask, "Who are the redeemed?" but rather, "Who is the Redeemer?" Who could possibly take such sinners and elevate them to a position of prominence and honor? Who could take those who are least deserving and raise them up with Christ, that they might be seated with Him on the Father's right hand?

BEING WITH CHRIST SHOULD BE OUR CONSUMING PASSION.

PLANNING NOW FOR THE FEAST TO COME

What are we to be doing now, on earth, during this time of courtship? We are engaged to our Bridegroom but the wedding is still off in the future. The apostle Paul, writing to the church in Corinth said, "I promised you to one husband, to Christ, so that I might present you as a pure virgin to him. But I am afraid that just as Eve was deceived by the serpent's cunning, your minds may somehow be led astray from your sincere and pure devotion to Christ" (2 Corinthians 11:2–3). Recall that in Jewish tradition, the long engagement was to prove the purity and faithfulness of each partner during the waiting period. Paul fears that during this time of engagement when we are waiting for the groom to take His bride to heaven, we might be lured into sin by other suitors. We might be sharing our affections with some other pleasure. We might be proving ourselves unfaithful to the covenant of engagement we have entered between us and the Bridegroom.

Every idol in our lives, whether a person or an unchecked desire for "the lust of the flesh, and the lust of the eyes, and the pride of life" (1 John 2:16 KJV) competes for our affection for the Bridegroom to whom we are engaged. If we are to be faithful, we have to be pure—wholly devoted to the one to whom we are betrothed.

Just think of an engaged couple, eagerly anticipating their wedding day. They are committed to being faithful to each other; they are growing closer in their understanding of each other and also, and most importantly, in their desire to be finally united without ever having to part. Just so, we should be developing a closer relationship with Jesus and we should experience the longing of two lovers who mark each day on the calendar as being "one day closer" to finally being able to wed their beloved. Being with Christ should be our consuming passion. As Luther said, "There are only two days: today and *that* day."

Finally a warning: Jesus told an interesting parable about a man who showed up for a wedding feast and didn't have the right garment, and so was instantly spotted and asked to leave (Matthew 22:11–13). Don't assume that you will arrive at the marriage supper just because you love Christ or serve Him. There must be a transfer of trust to Christ for salvation and the gift of righteousness we desperately need to gain entry into the heavenly portals. Without a proper garment of righteousness we cannot be saved.

Years ago under the presidency of the senior George H. W. Bush, I had the privilege of actually visiting the White House and I stood in the Oval Office. It was a holiday and the president was out of town. A secret service agent I had come to know told me that I and my two daughters who were with me could meet him and we could enter the White House together.

THE ANGELS LOOK AT US AND **SAY,** "OH, **YOU'RE WITH** *HIM?* GO ON IN."

We met him the next day and he took us past the other agents who instantly recognized him. They looked at us and then they looked at him and said, "Oh, you're with him? Just go on in." When we reached the steps of the White House, more Secret Service agents saw us and then looked at the agent beside us and they said, "Oh, you're with him? Go on in." And then when we walked down the hallway in the White House there was one more guard who stood at attention at the door of the Oval Office, but recognizing our escort, he allowed us in (though we were not allowed to go near the president's desk). We were at least able to say we had taken a step into the Oval Office!

Imagine with me that we all die, perhaps together. On the other side we meet Jesus, who is prepared to escort us all the way to the Father's house. Then visualize that along the way there are sentries of angels standing guard, protecting the way to the heavenly city. The angels look at us and say, "Oh, you're with Him? Go on in." We meet more angels who say, "Oh, you're with *Him?* Go on in."

And then in the distance we see the glory of God, and we are overwhelmed because God is more holy and more righteous and more pure than we ever dreamed. Suddenly we have a flashback, and we remember our sins. Some among us are burdened with a really dark past, having committed crimes of immorality and theft and selfishness. We look at ourselves and we say, "We can't go in! We *can't* go in!" But the angel at the door of the kingdom says, "You're with *Him.* Go on in," and so we are escorted all the way into the Father's house.

The Father then looks at the Son and says, "Thank You for bringing My children home, for I love them and want to be with them. And I have considered them carefully and find no fault in them." King Jesus has complete and unrestricted rights to enter heaven and appear before the Father, and so will we. *With Him,* we not only have unrestricted access but we are welcomed into the holy place of the Most High.

That is why we who are believers sing:

> Clothed in His righteousness alone
> Faultless to stand before the throne

We are welcomed to the wedding feast because we have the righteousness of Christ credited to us; we also have been appropriately judged for the way we have lived, and now we are also given a second suit of clothes, "the righteous acts of the saints." The one who sought us by grace, and brought us home by grace, now invites us to feast with Him by grace.

And, just to think, eternity has hardly begun!

NOTES

1. Stephen Davey, pastor of Colonial Baptist Church in Cary, North Carolina.

2. John R. W. Stott, *God's New Society: The Message of Ephesians* (Downers Grove, IL: InterVarsity Press, 1979), 82.

CHAPTER FOUR

THE KING
TOLERATES A RIVAL

*The Antichrist will be an attractive and charismatic
figure, a genius, a demon-controlled, devil-taught charmer
of men. He will have answers to the horrendous problems of
mankind. He will be all things to all men: a political statesman,
a social lion, a financial wizard, an intellectual giant, a
religious deceiver, a masterful orator, a gifted organizer. He will be
Satan's masterpiece of deception, the world's false messiah.
With boundless enthusiasm the masses will follow him and readily
enthrone him in their hearts as this world's savior and god.*
—John Phillips

In the Hofburg Library in Vienna there is a spear on display believed by many to be the one that was used by the Roman soldier who pierced Christ's side. When Adolf Hitler was in Vienna before his rise to power in Germany, he spent a great deal of time contemplating this Roman spear. He believed that this spear, encased behind glass, was authentic, even though there were forty-five other spears that some claim to be the one the Roman soldier used for the ghastly deed. Hitler's friends said that as he stared at that spear, he was engulfed in "ectoplasmic light" as he invited its spirit to possess him.

GERMANS WHO LIVED DURING THAT PERIOD OF TIME SAID THAT WE AS AMERICANS CAN NEVER UNDERSTAND THE EUPHORIC IMPACT HITLER HAD ON THEM.

Later on, when Hitler moved to Munich, he was drawn into the deepest levels of occult transformation. Dietrich Eckart, who was Hitler's mentor, claimed that Hitler was to be anointed the messiah. He wrote, "He shall dance, but I have written the tune, and because I have introduced him to the powers, I shall have had more impact on Germany than any other German." One of the observers said that Hitler's body was but the shell for the spirit that inhabited him.

HITLER AND ANTICHRIST

Why is it that when we speak about the Antichrist, Hitler comes to mind? We don't think of Stalin, or of Mao, each of whom also killed millions of people. We think of Hitler as a prototype of the Antichrist first, because he arose in Germany democratically (at least somewhat so) and he was adored by the German people. I have spoken to Germans who lived during that period of time, and they said that we as Americans can never understand the euphoric impact Hitler had on them. Skeptics would go to the great rallies in Nuremberg and would come back saying, "Our father, Adolf, who art in Nuremberg, the Third Reich, come." What a mesmerizing dictator he was!

We also think of Hitler as a prototype of the Antichrist because of his hatred for the Jews. The Antichrist, who will be more evil than Hitler, will also attempt to exterminate the Jewish people. This leader, blessed with modern technology, will commit evils that Hitler could only dream about. When he appears on the world stage, he will be speaking of peace but planning for war.

Finally, Hitler is a prototype of the Antichrist because he arose in Germany during a time of high inflation and economic chaos. In short order he stabilized the economy and put Germans back to work. His economic miracles made him an object of adoration among the disillusioned masses.

Antichrist will also arise on the world stage after an economic tsunami that will cause millions of desperate people to turn to a man who can lift them out of high unemployment, food shortages, and cultural chaos. As I write this, there is already talk about the need for just such an economic miracle worker. On October 24, 2011, the Vatican called for a radical reform of the world's financial systems, including the creation of a global political authority to manage the economy. The proposal by the Pontiff's Council for Justice and Peace calls for a new world economic order based on the "achievement of a universal common good." It is to ensure that reforms "must not damage the weakest economies while also achieving the distribution of the world's wealth."[1] The need for a one-world currency will be increasingly attractive in a world of economic instability. As I write this we are already facing a global economic crisis with nations in the world teetering on the brink of what could become an economic meltdown.

I've often wondered how the transition from the individual currencies to a worldwide single currency might come about. Recently I read a book titled *The World Crisis: The Path to the World Afterwards*, by Franck Biancheri, in which he details what he believes the G-20 has to do to bring stability after the world falls into its inevitable economic decline. He believes that a new international currency must be created. The individual nations will keep their present currency but will have to buy this new currency to conduct global trade. Thus, as I understand it, the value of each individual "basket of currencies" will fluctuate according to the economic health of each country. For example, as the American dollar declines, it will take more dollars to buy the new currency. Biancheri contends that this new benchmark currency "would only exist electronically, first as a unit of account, secondly, for trade between states and very large economic entities."[2] This, he believes, will be brought about voluntarily or by necessity when the world economy finally collapses.

ALTHOUGH I BELIEVE WE WILL BE IN HEAVEN WITH JESUS, ENJOYING HIS PRESENCE, IT MIGHT BE POSSIBLE FOR US TO KNOW OR EVEN SEE EVENTS UNFOLDING ON EARTH.

It does not take much imagination to realize that eventually the individual currencies will be abandoned in favor of simply accepting the benchmark international currency which will be recognized and accepted all over the world. Thus in order to buy so much as a loaf of bread, it will be necessary to deal in the Beast's accepted currency. And, as already indicated, these economic policies will force people to "worship the Beast" or be killed. The currency will be a symbol of allegiance to the one and only world ruler.

Once the church has been raptured, the Antichrist will appear. He may not appear immediately; it might take a few months or even a few years for nations to realign themselves on the world stage for Antichrist's crafty rise to power. Although I believe we will be in heaven with Jesus, enjoying His presence, it might be possible for us to know or even see events unfolding on earth. So after the rapture, various geopolitical events will arrange themselves in accordance with God's program to wrap up history according to biblical predictions.

When the world struggles to dig itself out of the depths of a catastrophic depression, it will turn to any man who has the charisma to convince the nations that he is able to bring stability and hope to a stricken chaotic world. One writer, referring back to Nazi Germany, says that this generation is already open to "an updated Fuehrer." There is a growing belief that different groups must coalesce to cause nations to surrender their nationalism in favor of a one-world government. Ervin Laszlo of the United Nations Institute for Training says that society must enter into a stage of "critical instability" to hasten the evolution of the new man at "the tail end of one civilization and the dawn of another." Given the fact that the economies of the world are interrelated, we can easily imagine that the world will reach a "critical mass of instability" and be ready for a world leader. Once the world is destabilized, Antichrist will seize power.

The prophet Daniel had inside information about both the immediate future and the more distant future when God would wrap up history. Proof that he was receiving his revelations from God is that some of his predictions have already come to pass. For example, he predicted the coming of Antiochus Epiphanes, who would come against the Jews and desecrate the temple. This was fulfilled centuries after Daniel's prediction when in about 170 BC Antiochus entered Jerusalem and desecrated the temple and attempted to exterminate the Jews. However, it is clear that Antiochus's career foreshadowed that of a future king, namely the Antichrist who would do more evil than Antiochus. This future ruler will have the audacity to "stand against the Prince of princes." He will be given his authority by Satan and use deception to ensnare the world in his schemes. In Daniel 8:23–25 we read:

> In the latter part of their reign, when rebels have become completely wicked, a stern-faced king, a master of intrigue, will arise. He will become very strong, but not by his own power. He will cause astounding devastation and will succeed in whatever he does. He will destroy the mighty men and the holy people. He will cause

deceit to prosper, and he will consider himself superior. When they feel secure, he will destroy many and take his stand against the Prince of princes. Yet he will be destroyed, but not by human power.

Yes, he will be *a master of intrigue; he will cause deceit to prosper!* His mesmerizing lies will cause the world to follow him. In desperation, the world will deify this new Caesar.

WHEN ANTICHRIST COPIES CHRIST

That word, *Antichrist*, has the prefix "anti" for a reason. He will serve as Satan's mouthpiece, Satan's emissary, and Satan's CEO. Everything Jesus does, Satan will try to copy, and do so with convincing distinction. I've seen some research that proposes as many as twenty similarities between Christ and Antichrist. For our purposes I shall just list seven ways in which Antichrist will try to mimic Jesus:

- Both claim to be God. Jesus made such claims when He was on earth; Antichrist will eventually take that honor to himself.
- Both make a covenant with Israel. Jesus referred to His as the "new covenant in his blood"; Antichrist will ratify a covenant with Israel guaranteeing the nation's security.
- Both appear in a temple. Jesus entered into the temple multiple times and chided those who were misusing it and not honoring it as a "house of prayer for all nations." Antichrist will enter into a newly built temple in Jerusalem and there proclaim himself to be God.
- Fourth, both are crowned and worshiped. Jesus ascended into heaven to reign as king; Antichrist, as we shall see, has "ten crowns on his horns" (Revelation 13:1). And he will demand the worship of the world.

- Fifth, both will perform signs and wonders. Jesus did so and Antichrist will do many miracles that will deceive many.
- Sixth, both have armies. Antichrist will eventually be fighting with other armies for the control of Jerusalem. Jesus will return with an army of angels and redeemed people to judge the world and establish His rule on earth.
- Both are put to death and then rise from the dead to the everlasting wonder of the world. Yes, whether Antichrist actually is dead or he only appears to be dead, either way, the world will believe that he has in fact died and believe that he has been dramatically raised from the dead. The evidence, however presented, will appear credible.

In the end, the Antichrist is exposed for the evil phony he is; Jesus is revealed not only as a conqueror but one who is just and true; an avenger but also a Savior for those who trust Him and His work. The one justly ends in everlasting torment; the other rules over the universe in great glory. The contrast between the two is infinite.

THE ANTICHRIST'S RISE TO POWER

As we give a brief overview of Antichrist's rise to power and tragically failed career, we must not get lost in the details but see the overall scheme of his designs and plans. We should marvel at his worldwide power and also his humiliating demise.

Let's begin with a New Testament description of Antichrist in Revelation 13:1–2.

And the dragon stood on the shore of the sea. And I saw a beast coming out of the sea. He had ten horns and seven heads, with ten crowns on his horns, and on each head a blasphemous name. The beast I saw resembled a leopard, but had feet like those of a bear and a mouth like that of a lion. The dragon gave the beast his power and his throne and great authority.

This beast is not a domesticated animal, but is ferocious, gruesome, and grotesque. How shall we interpret this hideous creature? We get our clues from the prophet Daniel who was given insight into the distant future. King Nebuchadnezzar had a dream of a statue representing the coming kingdoms of this world. Daniel's interpretation, granted to him by God, predicted the sequence of world empires till the end of time.

First, there would be Babylon (in existence in Daniel's time); then the Medo-Persian Empire would arise, then Greece, and finally the legs and the feet of the statue represent Rome. And as the interpretation continues, we learn that this kingdom—Rome—would be in existence when the Lord Jesus Christ returns to establish His kingdom. What this means is that the Roman Empire that faded away centuries ago will have to be revived in a final form, with ten "kings" or rulers (represented by ten toes).

So, in John's description, we know that the ten horns represent ten rulers who will serve him as part of his larger kingdom, and actually it is from one of these "kingdoms" that Antichrist will eventually arise. In a parallel passage, Daniel predicted that the Antichrist would arise as a "little horn" who will wage war against the saints "until the Ancient of Days came and pronounced judgment in favor of the saints of the Most High, and the time came when they possessed the kingdom" (Daniel 7:21–2). So from the ten horns a little horn arises and defeats three other "horns" and eventually gains control over ten horns and ten kingdoms.

The seven heads on the beast refer to a succession of different kingdoms: The leopard represents Greece, the bear represents the Medo-Persian Empire, and the lion symbolizes Babylon.

Again we turn to the book of Daniel to help us with this identification (see Daniel 7:1–6).

As we work our way through this complex vision, let's not forget the bottom line: Antichrist is both a person and a kingdom of unified states. So it appears that this conglomeration, representing the major kingdoms that have existed on the earth, will arise out of Europe (the revived Roman Empire). Let's summarize this teaching. (1) Antichrist will arise out of the ten toes (the revived Roman Empire) and (2) he will begin unobtrusively as "a little horn" but then shall (3) conquer all rivals and (4) he will wage war against God's people and (5) he shall be destroyed by God (the Ancient of Days) and (6) his territory will be given to the saints of the Most High.

THE POSSIBLE ROLE OF A MUSLIM MESSIAH

We all have heard of the speech given by President Mahmoud Ahmadinejad of Iran back in 2005 when he spoke of the coming of the Shiite Messiah, al-Mahdi. It is believed that this man will emerge during a time of worldwide chaos, wielding both an economic and a military sword to bring peace and justice to the earth.

In his book *Islam: The Cloak of Antichrist*, Jack Smith argues that the description of this Islamic messiah and the anticipated events that surround his coming fit perfectly with the biblical prophecies. He gives reasons to believe that Daniel's interpretation of King Nebuchadnezzar's dream actually predicted the coming of the Islamic Empire and not the revival of the ancient Roman Empire as frequently taught. Smith argues that what many see as the revived form of the Roman Empire is actually a prediction of the coming of the religious empire of worldwide Islam.

Belief in the coming of the Messiah known as al-Mahdi traces back to AD 872 when Muhammad b. Hasan was born. He was the son of the Eleventh Imam of the branch of Islam known as the Shi'ahs. Tradition says that when the father feared his son (who was expected to be the Twelfth Imam) might be killed by the rival Sunni Muslims, the boy was hidden at the age of seven. By divine command he went into a state of "occultation," where he is still hidden to this day, although he is still in contact with his followers and spokesmen on earth. According to this belief, he did not die but continues in this hidden state ready to be revealed at the appropriate time. Those who accept this scenario are known as "twelvers" because they believe that this man who should have been the twelfth imam was denied this honor because of the opposition of the Sunnis. But he will eventually be vindicated when he is revealed to bring the world peace and justice.

Smith goes into great detail to show that the teachings about this Muslim Messiah parallel the description of Antichrist in many unexpected ways. For example, the Beast who is Antichrist is described as someone who "was" (Revelation 17:8), and now "is not" (17:8, 11) and "will come up out of the Abyss" (17:8). Just so, this imam "was" (he was born in 872); he "is not" (he has been in "occultation" or hiding for centuries); and he is about to "come out of the abyss" that, is to be revealed. Then he will go into destruction. The *Abyss* is used in the Scriptures as a place where demons are incarcerated. Evidently this king will not merely be human, but will appear in human form. He will be the prince of the Abyss, Satan, disguised as a man.

A strong objection to the idea that the Antichrist could be the al-Mahdi is that Islam is vehemently opposed to worshiping a man—any man. In Islam, God is distant and unknowable, and to worship a man would be high blasphemy. Smith addresses this issue by saying that it is clear that the Beast of Revelation 13 is a demonic being who gets his power and authority from Satan (Revelation 13:2). Thus when the world worships this beast, they think they are actually worshiping their deity, who is Satan in disguise. In fact, it is expressly stated, "Men worshiped the dragon because he had given authority to the beast, and they also worshiped the beast and asked, 'Who is like the beast? Who can make war against him?'" (v. 4). Therefore Smith believes that this "beast" is actually the worship of a false satanic god.

Smith makes the interesting point that there are only three beings who are judged and thrown into hell without dying: (1) the Beast; (2) the false prophet; and (3) finally Satan (see Revelation 19:20–21; 20:1–3). This is further proof, he reasons, that the Beast and false prophet are not actually men but demonic beings. Humans have to die and be resurrected with indestructible bodies before they can be thrown into hell; only satanic beings are thrown directly into the fires of hell, bypassing death.

We must also keep in mind that the al-Mahdi is actually believed to be a supernatural creature who is beyond human. So for Muslims to worship this man might, in their view, be like worshiping Allah who has sent him and given him authority to bring peace on the earth. His first assignment will be to destroy rival religions (especially Christianity) and impose Islam throughout the world, fulfilling the prediction of Muhammad himself, that there will be no place on earth where Allah will not be worshiped. Sharia law will be imposed, and woe to those who refuse to bow to this Islamic leader.[2]

THE BOTTOM LINE IS THAT WE DO NOT KNOW WHO THE ANTICHRIST WILL BE, BUT REGARDLESS OF HIS RELIGIOUS LEANINGS, HE WILL, FOR A TIME, TERRORIZE THE POPULATION OF THE WORLD.

The rich symbolism of the book of Revelation is subject to various interpretations. Whether Smith's minority view of the end time events will be widely received remains to be seen. In the following pages I will present the more widely held view that Antichrist will be an actual man who arises out of the Roman Empire and will eventually demand worship. He will make a covenant with Israel, and although he will have the same worldwide thirst for control as the predicted al-Mahdi, it is not necessary that he be seen as a Muslim messiah intent on bringing the world under the heel of Sharia law. It is indeed unlikely that a Muslim messiah would ever sign a peace treaty with Israel.

The bottom line is that we do not know who the Antichrist will be, but regardless of his religious leanings, he will, for a time, terrorize the population of the world. But fortunately, only for a few years because the glorious triumph of Jesus is assured.

THE ANTICHRIST'S CAREER

Let's continue with a description of the Antichrist's rise to power and his subsequent temporary victories in ruling the world.

HIS SPECTACULAR RESURRECTION

I'm not sure of the exact time in his career, but the Antichrist will stage a resurrection. We read, "One of its heads seemed to have a mortal wound, but its mortal wound was healed, and the whole earth marveled as they followed the beast. And they worshiped the dragon, for he had given his authority to the beast, and they worshiped the beast, saying, 'Who is like the beast, and who can fight against it?'" (Revelation 13:3–4 ESV). Whether or not the beast has a literal resurrection, he will look as if he has died and then come back to full strength. The response of the people will be that this is not just a man, but God.

Some Bible teachers believe that he will actually die because the phrase that is used, "a mortal wound" is the same expression used of Jesus—"a Lamb, looking as if it had been slain" (Revelation 5:6). Of course we know that Jesus actually died, so perhaps the Antichrist will actually die. However, I think it is clear that Satan cannot raise people from the dead unless there is a very special power given to him by God. So, perhaps it only *appears* as if Antichrist actually dies and in some mysterious manner he deceives people about his death and apparent resurrection.

Stephen Davey, a preacher friend of mine, says, "Just visualize it. This man is a world leader and somebody assassinates him. He's there in a coffin in some great rotunda in the Middle East, and thousands of people are lining up, and all the television cameras are on his corpse, and then suddenly he wiggles and crawls out of the coffin and says, 'I'm your Messiah.'"

DEVOID OF DISCERNMENT, THE MASSES WILL SAY, "THIS IS OUR MAN!"

Who would dare challenge someone who was dead and now is alive? Given our Western fondness for spirituality, it is not difficult to see why a gullible world will be ready for such a leader. Devoid of discernment, the masses will say, "This is our man!" Jesus claimed to be the Messiah, but he was seen by only a few of his disciples; this man rises from the dead for all the world to see! Thanks to television, in a mockery of the prediction about Jesus, it can be said, "and every eye shall see him"!

No wonder the world asks, "Who is like the beast, and who can fight against it?" (Revelation 13:3–4 ESV). And, the world is so mesmerized by the Beast that they worship the dragon (Satan) who gave his power to the Beast. In Revelation chapter 12 Satan is called the red dragon because he is filled with the blood of the saints. Thankfully, in that chapter we read an intriguing account of how Michael the archangel and his angels threw the dragon and his angels out of heaven (vv. 7–12). But for a short time he will receive the worship he craves.

HE SIGNS A PEACE TREATY

The teaching that Antichrist will sign a peace treaty with Israel, guaranteeing the security of that tiny country, is based on Daniel 9:27, where we read that "He [the context makes it clear that the antecedent is Antichrist] will confirm a covenant with many for

one 'seven' [seven years]. In the middle of the 'seven' he will put
an end to sacrifice and offering. And on a wing of the temple he
will set up an abomination that causes desolation, until the end
that is decreed is poured out on him." Obviously this verse begs
to be interpreted.

He will "confirm a covenant with many for one 'seven'"; that
is, he will make a covenant that will last seven years. By then he
will have such stature that when this treaty is signed, the world
will give a sigh of relief, believing that peace has finally come
to the Middle East and for that matter, to the world. He will be
respected internationally and will apply enough pressure on Israel's neighbors to broker peace and restrain their lust for war.

Keep in mind that the signing of the peace treaty will be the
beginning of what is called the great tribulation. However, the
first three and one-half years will be a time of remarkable calm
as the world believes that its new leader actually has the ability
to maintain a global peace arrangement. Nationalism will be in
check and the world will coalesce around the new messiah who
will give evidence that his vision for peace will triumph. There
will be a consensus that the world at last can destroy its weapons, because the nations will have agreed to live in peace under
this man's mesmerizing influence. However, behind the doves of
peace will be the weapons of war.

But there is another aspect to Daniel's prophecy.

HIS CLAIM TO DEITY

And what might the "abomination that causes desolation" refer
to? With peace supposedly coming to the region, a temple will
be built in Jerusalem. We don't know if it will be built next to the
Muslim Dome of the Rock, the surrounding area, or if the massive
Dome will already have been shattered by an earthquake, but
there will be a temple, perhaps a small one, built on the temple

mount. So the most likely interpretation of the phrase "an abomination that causes desolation" is that after Antichrist makes his seven-year covenant with Israel (seven weeks in the Hebrew text) and then three and one-half years later (in the middle of the week), he breaks his covenant, puts an end to the sacrifices taking place in the newly rebuilt temple, and declares that he is God. This is exactly what Jesus refers to in Matthew 24:15 (to be considered in more detail in the next chapter of this book).

Paul writes about the same event: "He will oppose and will exalt himself over everything that is called God or is worshiped, so that he sets himself up in God's temple, proclaiming himself to be God" (2 Thessalonians 2:4). So, this future ruler will not only be used by Satan, but will compete for the position of God, demanding the worship of the world.

Satan's desire throughout the ages is to duplicate everything that Jesus has ever done and to receive the worship of the world. That's why he said to Jesus, " 'All this I will give you,' he said, 'if you will bow down and worship me'" (Matthew 4:9). Satan longs to be worshiped, and in the Antichrist he will have somebody in place who will gladly receive that worship from the people of the world. As they worship the Antichrist, they will worship the one who gave him his power, namely the devil, the great dragon.

THE ANTICHRIST RULES THE WORLD

The Antichrist will use fear to rule the world. Some of the biblical descriptions of his role should give us the chills. "The beast was given a mouth to utter proud words and blasphemies and to exercise his authority for forty-two months" (Revelation 13:5). Why forty-two months? That's three and a half years. The Antichrist declares himself to be God and he rules the world for the next three and one-half years until the seven years end and Jesus returns. He will be given a mouth, a very big mouth, filled with evil and blasphemy against God until King Jesus comes to destroy him.

At that time there will be a one-world religion, namely Antichrist worship. We continue, "He was given power to make war against the saints and to conquer them" (v. 7). This does not mean that the Antichrist could defeat believers spiritually, but he will physically persecute and kill those who do not take his mark. This will be a very difficult time to maintain loyalty to Christ. The price for following Jesus will be martyrdom.

Just try to visualize this: "He was given authority over every tribe, people, language and nation. All inhabitants of the earth will worship the beast—all whose names have not been written in the book of life belonging to the Lamb that was slain from the creation of the world" (vv. 7–8). Chilling.

People will say, "We have found our Messiah. We have found the answer to the world's complex problems and search for peace. Here he is." Multiplied millions bow to him and believe.

HE REVEALS HIS SATANIC TRINITY

The one-world religion will be enforced by a one-world economy. In order to do this, Antichrist will enlist the help of another beast whose presence completes the satanic trinity and helps unify the world under one currency in order to enforce universal worship of the one ruler.

God exists in a Trinity, so it should be no surprise that Satan, who wants to duplicate the Almighty, also has his "trinity." We have been introduced to the dragon, who is Satan (corresponding to God the Father); we have been introduced to the Beast (corresponding to God the Son); and now we find a description of a third member of this unholy triad, a false prophet, who directs people to worship the Beast (recall that this is the ministry of the Holy Spirit in the *Holy* Trinity).

Then I saw another beast, coming out of the earth. He had two horns like a lamb, but he spoke like a dragon. He exercised all the authority of the first beast on his behalf, and made the earth and its inhabitants worship the first beast, whose fatal wound had been healed. And he performed great and miraculous signs, even causing fire to come down from heaven to earth in full view of men. Because of the signs he was given power to do on behalf of the first beast, he deceived the inhabitants of the earth. He ordered them to set up an image in honor of the beast who was wounded by the sword and yet lived. He was given power to give breath to the image of the first beast, so that it could speak and cause all who refused to worship the image to be killed. He also forced everyone, small and great, rich and poor, free and slave, to receive a mark on his right hand or on his forehead, so that no one could buy or sell unless he had the mark, which is the name of the beast or the number of his name. (Revelation 13:11–17)

We should gasp at the audacity of Satan. His trinity tries to duplicate the Holy Trinity, and in the process forms a triad of unimaginable deception and evil. As this false prophet forces people to worship the Beast, he confirms his role with "signs and wonders" even as Paul predicted, "The coming of the lawless one will be in accordance with the work of Satan displayed in all kinds of counterfeit miracles, signs and wonders, and in every sort of evil that deceives those who are perishing. They perish because they refused to love the truth and so be saved" (2 Thessalonians 2:9–10). The phrase "signs and wonders" is similar to that used of the miracles of the apostles (Acts 2:22), showing that Satan's ability to duplicate the miracles of God will be impressive, and a gullible world, desperate to believe what is false, will embrace these deceptions.

An image is erected, and "He was given power to give breath to the image of the first beast, so that it could speak" (Revelation

13–15). Perhaps through trickery and direct demonic power, the image is able to speak and insist that those who do not worship the Beast be slain. No one can buy or sell without the "mark of the beast" either on the right hand or on the forehead. "So that no one could buy or sell unless he had the mark, which is the name of the beast or the number of his name. This calls for wisdom. If anyone has insight, let him calculate the number of the beast, for it is man's number. His number is 666" (vv. 17–18). This could be some kind of tattoo, and it might be enforced by a computer chip or other advanced technology.

Now, this certainly does call for wisdom! Throughout history all kinds of explanations have been given for 666. People have toyed around with various names, assigning numbers to each letter coming up with a total of 666. Regardless of the interpretation, we know that with computer chips it is easy to see how a cashless currency could be implemented worldwide. Each time you made a purchase, your account would simply be debited. There could be no secret transactions of cash as there are today, especially in drug deals and other illegal activities. Every purchase, expenditure, and money earned would be recorded and known by those who are assigned to keep people under control. Thus, Antichrist would enforce "economic equality."

Starvation will drive millions to desperation, willing to worship the beast in order to live. If you want to eat, you have to submit to Antichrist; if you want your children to have food, you must swear personal allegiance to the only man who is able to save the world. The unconverted will worship anyone who promises them economic stability coupled with peace.

Hitler could only have dreamed of this kind of control for the inhabitants of his "kingdom." Antichrist will be able to implement a worldwide religious and economic system that will force compliance. The choice will be stark: worship the Beast or be killed.

THE ANTICHRIST'S END

For the end of the Beast's career we must return to a later chapter in the book of Revelation. "Then I saw the beast and the kings of the earth and their armies gathered together to make war against the rider on the horse and his army" (Revelation 19:19). And who is the rider who comes to make war with the beast? In context, we see it is the Lord Jesus Christ who comes to conquer. Follow the Beast and you end in hell, the lake that burns with sulfur.

> But the beast was captured, and with him the false prophet who had performed the miraculous signs on his behalf. With these signs he had deluded those who had received the mark of the beast and worshiped his image. The two of them were thrown alive into the fiery lake of burning sulfur. The rest of them were killed with the sword that came out of the mouth of the rider on the horse, and all the birds gorged themselves on their flesh. (Revelation 19:20–21)

The Beast (Antichrist) and the false prophet will actually be cast into the lake of fire before Satan joins them. Satan will be bound for a thousand years, and then after this he will join the Beast and the false prophet in the lake of fire, "and the devil, who deceived them, was thrown into the lake of burning sulfur, where the beast and the false prophet had been thrown. They will be tormented day and night for ever and ever" (Revelation 20:10).

Satan knows the address of his final destination. He can read the book of Revelation just as well as we can. That's why when he is thrown out of heaven (probably in the middle of the tribulation period), he is furious because he knows "his time is short."

Satan and his puppet win for a few years. Jesus wins for eternity.

LESSONS FOR TODAY

What should we learn from this coming event? First, we desperately need spiritual discernment. When Antichrist appears, he will be accepted because of his false miracles and lies. Today many people—including Christians—do not know how to distinguish true miracles from the "signs and wonders" that are sometimes claimed by evangelists of various kinds. I agree that sometimes it is difficult to distinguish the true from the false, but usually there are telltale signs we must watch for. Some people are so ignorant of the Bible and the seductions of modern spirituality that they will attend a séance, or seek a medium who can help them make contact with the dead. Or think of the millions who are followers of Oprah Winfrey's guru, Eckhart Tolle. Here is occultism packaged for the masses. Antichrist will most probably introduce himself to the world as a man of "deep spirituality" and for this he will be adored and followed.

WE SHOULD NEVER INTERPRET THE PATIENCE OF GOD AS THE WEAKNESS OF GOD.

In this terrifying scenario given in the book of Revelation, we also can be comforted by God's sovereignty. When the Scripture says that the Beast was given authority to rule for forty-two months, it is God who determines that length of time. And if God says it is forty-two months, it cannot be forty-three!

Jesus will slay Antichrist "with the breath of his mouth" (2 Thessalonians 2:8). Jesus will just have to breathe and Antichrist and his forces will be routed, destroyed, killed awaiting a resurrection unto judgment. We should never interpret the patience of God as the weakness of God. God allows evil to run its course for His own purposes and His own glory.

Finally, let us remember God's power to sustain His saints in the midst of a holocaust of global proportions. Take a glance back over Revelation 13:8. "All inhabitants of the earth will worship the beast—all whose names have not been written in the book of life belonging to the Lamb that was slain from the creation of the world." Will God be able to sustain those who come to faith in Christ during the tribulation period? It appears that way. Despite the economic and religious pressure, those who belong to Christ will not worship the Beast, *even if they see their children starve.*

Hitler believed that if you go to a rally as a skeptic and see and hear 100,000 people shout the same slogans, you will either change your mind or you will keep silent. It is almost impossible for one person or a few people to withstand the threat of death that comes from a ruler who has the adoration of the world at his fingertips. But God will grant His people the strength to do so. They will overcome him "by the blood of the Lamb and by the word of their testimony" (Revelation 12:11).

There is a Book of Life that has existed from the creation of the world. Those whose names are listed there belong to the Lamb. If you are a believer today, your name was written in the Book of Life for as long as God has existed (Revelation 13:8).

Finally, we should make sure that our names are written in this Book of Life. There is only one way to find out: if we come to Jesus and receive Him as our Savior, we can be assured that our name is written in God's book. Assurance is not only possible, but available to all who will believe God's promises of redemption for themselves.

Most often when I fly on an airplane I have a confirmed ticket. But I've also flown "standby" and there is a difference! On standby you are not sure whether there will be a seat for you on the plane; you are nervous, apprehensive, speaking to the agent, hoping that a confirmed passenger has canceled. If you are number 4 on the waiting list, you wait patiently as other standby passengers go on ahead of you.

But with a ticket, I know I have a seat reserved—10B, for example. So I can wait at the lounge with patience and be totally relaxed. Just so, you can have a confirmed ticket by faith in Christ; you can know there is a place reserved for you in glory. "Yet to all who received him, to those who believed in his name, he gave the right to become children of God" (John 1:12). Assurance comes by trusting Christ alone for salvation, and rejecting all confidence in our good works. When we are thus "born again" the Holy Spirit indwells us to confirm our security (Romans 8:15–17).

Those whose names are written in the Lamb's Book of Life will be welcomed into heaven even if they must pass through the tribulation. Not even the Beast can erase their names from the Book of Life. "My sheep listen to my voice; I know them, and they follow me. I give them eternal life, and they shall never perish; no one can snatch them out of my hand. My Father, who has given them to me, is greater than all; no one can snatch them out of my Father's hand. I and the Father are one" (John 10:27–30).

With the signing of the covenant, Antichrist will usher in an initial time of peace, but in time great tribulation will follow. It is to the tribulation itself that we now turn our attention.

For those on the earth, unimaginable suffering will have arrived.

NOTES

1. "Vatican Calls for New World Economy Order," published October 24, 2011.

2. Franck Biancheri, *The World Crisis: The Path to the World Afterwards* (Nice, France: Anticipolis Editions, 2010).

3. Jack Smith, *Islam: The Cloak of Antichrist* (Enumclaw, WA: Winepress, 2011).

CHAPTER FIVE

THE KING JUDGES
THOSE LEFT BEHIND

There are major, unprecedented forces at work right now
that seem to be, of their own volition, moving us toward some
manner of cataclysmic shift. Whatever name people give it, the end
of all that we have ever known is nearer than it has ever been.
–Robert Stearns

Judgment.

The word is not popular in our vocabulary. We'd like to think that God's love will cancel His judgment. We want a God we do not have to fear; a God who understands our weaknesses, overlooks our sins, and exists solely for our happiness. However, such a God is the figment of our imagination, not the deity revealed in the Bible. And Jesus, who is commonly thought of as "meek and mild," is also revealed in Scripture as a fierce judge who will not spare the guilty.

In the previous chapter we were introduced to the Antichrist

MANY PEOPLE MINIMIZE THE TRIBULATION BECAUSE THEY SPIRITUALIZE IT RATHER THAN CONSIDER IT A LITERAL ASPECT OF GOD'S FUTURE PLAN.

whose treaty with Israel is the starting point of the great tribulation. Now, we will take a careful look at what Jesus has to say about this period of time, to gain a better grasp of God's intention and purposes for this horrific time of suffering to come on Planet Earth.

Many people minimize the tribulation because they spiritualize it rather than consider it a literal aspect of God's future plan. They argue that the church has always gone through tribulation, so why should we think that some future tribulation will be unique? Some Bible teachers even suggest it has already happened. Like other doctrines of prophecy, this one has stirred considerable debate.

Yes, there has always been tribulation, but the earth has never experienced the level of catastrophe we will discuss in this chapter. The Old Testament predicted a day of great trouble on the earth. The Lord God said He would scatter Israel and then would bring them together, saying, "When you are in distress and all these things have happened to you, then in later days you will return to the Lord your God and obey him" (Deuteronomy 4:30). This theme is even more developed in the book of Daniel:

> At that time Michael, the great prince who protects your people, will arise. There will be a time of distress such as has not happened from the beginning of nations until then. But at that time your people—everyone whose name is found written in the book—will be delivered. Multitudes who sleep in the dust of the earth will awake: some to everlasting life, others to shame and everlasting contempt. (Daniel 12:1–2)

Daniel predicts (1) that there will be a time of distress or tribulation "such as has not happened from the beginning of nations," a clear reference to the coming great tribulation. He also affirms that (2) not all the Jews ("your people") will experience deliverance but only those whose names are written in "the book" that is, the book of the redeemed. Then (3) there will be two resurrections, those who are raised to everlasting life and those who are raised to everlasting shame and contempt. In the New Testament it becomes clear that these resurrections do not happen simultaneously, but are separated by at least a thousand years. This will be clarified in a later chapter.

Yes, there is a day coming when great tribulation will come on the earth, such as has not been seen in all of history. Jesus confirmed this, and we must give His teaching careful thought.

THE PURPOSES OF THE TRIBULATION

Our focus in this chapter will be on the prophecies given by Jesus in Matthew 24:1–35, but before we investigate these predictions, I want to share with you some of the purposes of the great tribulation. Why does Scripture speak about this frightful event? What is God trying to accomplish during this time of unparalleled trouble? Here are a few of its purposes:

> WE DON'T THINK OF A LAMB AS BEING FILLED WITH WRATH, BUT THIS JESUS—THIS LAMB—WILL BE UNLEASHING HIS JUDGMENT ON THE WORLD.

First, during the last three and one-half years, God will finally unleash His wrath on the earth because sin will be rampant. In Revelation we have this description of people calling on the mountains and rocks to fall on them to shield them from the wrath of God: "Fall on us and hide us from the face of him who sits on the throne and from the wrath of the Lamb! For the great day of their wrath has come, and who can stand?" (Revelation 6:16–17). Imagine the phrase, "the wrath of the Lamb." We don't think of a lamb as being filled with wrath, but this Jesus—this Lamb—will be unleashing His judgment on the world. "Why is God so angry?" He's angry because, by and large, the world has turned its back on the salvation He offers. As the tribulation begins, almost the whole world is preparing to worship the Antichrist, all except those who are written in the Book of Life, will worship this false messiah (Revelation 13:8).

Today we are ripening for judgment. To take but one example, God hates immorality, and in the Bible homosexuality is singled out as the most egregious example of such conduct. While we must be sympathetic with those in the church who struggle with same-sex attraction, we must also realize that the radical homosexual agenda with its corruption of marriage is a sign that we are approaching a time of unparalleled wrath.[1] A friend of mine has pointed out that today the homosexual movement, which represents 2–3 percent of the population, has become a global political power with greater influence in the courtrooms and legislatures of the world than the church of Jesus Christ!

Homosexuals have veto power over everything that is presented on television, everything taught in our schools, and everything approved by our lawmakers. Meanwhile, the church of Jesus Christ mutely stands aside in the face of same-sex marriages, the indoctrination of schoolchildren, and a media awash in pro-homosexual propaganda. We appear paralyzed by the fear of incurring the wrath of the homosexual community and their powerful allies—the courts and the media.

The Bible is not silent about this. We all know the sin of Sodom and Gomorrah was rampant homosexuality, evidently accompanied by pedophilia and a willingness to commit rape. We read, "All the men from every part of the city of Sodom—both young and old—surrounded the house. They called to Lot, "Where are the men who came to you tonight? Bring them out to us so that we can have sex with them" (Genesis 19:4–5). Even the young men had been perverted, joining the older men in craving sex with Lot's guests. If Lot had acquiesced to their insistent demands, they obviously would have tried to forcibly sexualize these men whether they wanted such a relationship or not.

In the New Testament, we discover that Sodom is a picture of the coming future judgment. "In a similar way, Sodom and Gomorrah and the surrounding towns gave themselves up to sexual immorality and perversion. They serve as an example of those who suffer *the punishment of eternal fire*" (Jude 1:7, italics added). Peter echoes a similar thought: "He condemned the cities of Sodom and Gomorrah by burning them to ashes, and made them *an example of what is going to happen to the ungodly*" (2 Peter 2:6, italics added). Clearly, the judgment of Sodom and Gomorrah was primarily for their homosexuality as Jude teaches, rather than, as some would have us believe, that they were judged simply because of their lack of hospitality and greed described by Ezekiel 16:48–49.

In blatant defiance of God, two witnesses that God will send during the tribulation period (possibly Moses and Elijah) are violently killed for the message they proclaim. The victors gloat over their dead bodies, as Revelation describes, "Their bodies will lie in the street of the great city, which is figuratively called Sodom and Egypt, where also their Lord was crucified" (11:8). Why is Jerusalem, under Antichrist's rule, figuratively called *Sodom* and *Egypt*? Sodom represents rampant sexual perversion and Egypt represents slavery. These evils will be widespread when God's wrath is poured out on Planet Earth.

And yet, lest we point fingers at Sodom and Gomorrah, we must remember that Jesus said that the inhabitants of these cities are less culpable than those who have more opportunity to repent than they had (Matthew 11:23–24). No doubt the fire that destroyed Sodom and Gomorrah is but a microcosm of an even more fierce judgment that will be unleashed during the great tribulation because this generation (whether homosexual or heterosexual) is sinning against much more spiritual light and opportunity.

Not surprisingly, amid hailstones from heaven and rivers turning into blood, we read, "The rest of mankind that were not killed by these plagues still did not repent of the work of their hands; they did not stop worshiping demons, and idols of gold, silver, bronze, stone and wood—idols that cannot see or hear or walk. Nor did they repent of their murders, their magic arts, their sexual immorality or their thefts" (Revelation 9:20–21). Even suffering God's wrath did not motivate them to leave their idolatry, violence, and immorality. Some will repent; most will not.

The second reason for the great tribulation will be to prepare Israel to enter into the kingdom age. Some Jews will become believers in Christ as their Messiah during this period, and they will live to enter what is called the promised millennial kingdom. In fact, Jeremiah wrote, "How awful that day will be! None will be like it. It will be a time of trouble for Jacob, but he will be saved out of it" (Jeremiah 30:7). Paul said in Romans, "so all Israel will be saved" (Romans 11:26).

THERE WILL BE A REMNANT OF JEWISH PEOPLE WHO WILL SURVIVE THE TRIBULATION AND RECEIVE JESUS AS THE MESSIAH.

Zechariah gives us this description of the nation's future salvation, "And I will pour out on the house of David and the inhabitants of Jerusalem a spirit of grace and supplication. They will look on me, the one they have pierced, and they will mourn for him as one mourns for an only child, and grieve bitterly for him as one grieves for a firstborn son" (12:10). There will be a remnant of Jewish people who will survive the tribulation and receive Jesus as the Messiah when He returns with the saints to judge the earth and to establish His kingdom. These believing Jews, along with many Gentiles, will join together to enter the millennial kingdom where Christ Himself shall rule. The great tribulation sets up the events that make this scenario come to pass.

Then there is a final reason for the great tribulation—to show Jesus Christ's total triumph over Satan. During this great tribulation, Satan is no longer working undercover. He is described as the red dragon who has been cast out of heaven. In his fury, he will do all the damage that he can to rail at God and His people. As we learned in the previous chapter, at some point it will appear as if his man, the Antichrist, is winning, but in the end he will suffer a humiliating loss and be cast into the lake of fire, where he will be tormented day and night forever. The tribulation will prove that the contest will not even be close. Jesus will win, despite fierce opposition.

Keep in mind that during this time, we as believers will be with Christ in heaven, having been raptured (1 Thessalonians 4:13–18). So, as we read the vivid description of the horrors of the tribulation, we can be thankful that if pretribulationism is correct—and I believe it is—we shall be with Christ while these terrifying events transpire on earth. Paul tells us that we should "wait for his Son from heaven, whom he raised from the dead— Jesus, *who rescues us from the coming wrath*" (1 Thessalonians 1:10, italics added).

ISRAEL, THE FOCUS

With this as our background, let's consider the prophecies of Jesus in Matthew 24. He and His disciples were on the Mount of Olives overlooking the temple area. Jesus begins the conversation. "Do you see all these things? . . . I tell you the truth, not one stone here will be left on another; every one will be thrown down" (24:1–2).

The disciples then asked Him, "When will this happen, and what will be the sign of your coming and of the end of the age?"

(v. 3). Jesus, in effect, ignores their first question about when these things will take place, and instead launches into this discussion of the signs of His coming and the end of the age.

We should notice in passing that this account has some parallels with a similar narrative in the gospel of Luke where Jesus talks about the coming destruction of Jerusalem in AD 70 (Luke 21:5–24). This has made some students of the Bible teach that the events of Matthew 24 are also past history, and that Jesus is not speaking about the great tribulation but rather is simply referring to the destruction of the temple by the Romans. However, it seems clear that the destruction of the city by the Romans in AD 70 is actually a preview of a similar, but much greater destruction that is still to take place during the tribulation period.

In the Matthew account, Jesus is definitely referring to the future tribulation and not merely the coming of the Romans to capture the city in AD 70. He includes events that have never happened; for example, at no time in history has the gospel of the kingdom been proclaimed to the whole world (v. 14). Also, Jesus predicted, "For then there will be great distress, unequaled from the beginning of the world until now—and never to be equaled again" (v. 21). This statement is further proof that Jesus is not just describing the destruction of Jerusalem under the Romans in AD 70. That was a terrible time of starvation and the death of hundreds of thousands of Jews, but it was not as destructive as the Nazi holocaust with the torture and death of six million Jews. So the words that there will be "great distress" (tribulation) so much so that it will never be "equaled again" could not simply be a reference to the first-century destruction of Jerusalem. There have been times of distress much worse than that.

Think of the tribulation in three stages. First, the tribulation begins with the signing for a covenant with Israel. This agreement does bring peace and a measure of stability to the world for the first three and one-half years of the tribulation. Second, there is the dramatic event when Antichrist goes into the temple that will have been built in Jerusalem and proclaims himself to be God, beginning his pogrom against the Jews. This three-and-one-half-year period is the most terrible time of "the great tribulation" and is also when the seals, the bowls, and the trumpet judgments of Revelation are hurled upon the earth. Third, there is the battle of Armageddon, which ends with the glorious return of Christ.

Are the signs Jesus mentioned signs we should be watching for today? Yes and no. Strictly speaking, they are signs that will precede the glorious coming of Jesus with His saints; they are events that will transpire before Jesus comes to establish His kingdom. In other words, they are events that that will take place after the rapture of the church at a later time when the second stage of Christ's return takes place.

However, it is certainly possible that we will see the beginning of these signs even before the rapture. Think of it this way: The traffic signs that guide travelers as they near Chicago become more numerous as drivers get nearer to the city. Although the signs within the city are intended only for those who cross the border into the city proper, similar signs can already be seen along the highway. Just so, the predictions Jesus made are to take place after the rapture, but even before the rapture we can see indications that His return might not be far away.

In passing, we should notice that Matthew 24 is very Jewish. It speaks candidly about Jerusalem, the temple, the surrounding area of Judea, etc. Nothing is said about the church in this chapter. We can assume with a degree of confidence that the reason is because the church is nowhere in sight; the church has been raptured and we all are with Jesus. We've already discussed our arrival in the air with Christ and that subsequently we will all appear at the judgment seat of Christ. And sometime after that, we will be ushered into the marriage supper of the Lamb.

Jesus now speaks about a period in history when the Jews once again will become the centerpiece of God's program. There are still Old Testament promises made to the patriarchs and ratified by the prophets that need to be fulfilled. God picks up where the Old Testament era left off. Clearly, God is not finished with the Jewish nation, and Jerusalem remains the city where history as we know it will end.

THE SIGNS OF HIS COMING

Now let's look at the signs. "Watch out that no one deceives you. For many will come in my name, claiming, 'I am the Christ,' and will deceive many" (vv. 4–5). Obviously, this is a sign that is already happening today. There are many different "Jesuses" that are available to the masses. We have a Mormon Jesus; we have a New Age Jesus; we have a do-it-yourself Jesus; a cut-and-paste Jesus. People have different "Jesuses," but after the rapture, this sign will become even more evident. Many will say, "I am the Christ," preparing the populations for a huge worldwide deception.

WARS AND FAMINES AND EARTHQUAKES

Second, Jesus predicts there will be wars and rumors of wars. "You will hear of wars and rumors of wars, but see to it that you are not alarmed. Such things must happen, but the end is still to come" (v. 6). As the tribulation intensifies, warfare will become even more common than it is today. Eventually, the great tribulation will end with the battle of Armageddon.

Third, Jesus predicts famine. Hunger and starvation are nothing new. Today's statistics are overwhelming, but the terrible situation will become worse:

- Every 3.6 seconds someone dies of hunger—5 percent of them are children.
- 24,000 people die every day from starvation or malnutrition.
- Even in the richest country in the world, the United States, over ten million people suffer from hunger.
- Malnutrition, as measured by stunting of growth, affects 32.5 percent of children in developing countries.[1]

While starvation and famines exist today, the famine Jesus predicts during the great tribulation will outweigh them all. It is astonishing to think that despite the power exercised by a future global leader called the Antichrist, millions will live without the ability to even feed themselves. Times will be hard and food scarce.

Fourth, Jesus predicts there will be earthquakes in various places. While I'm told the number of earthquakes is increasing, this might simply reflect the fact that today we have better methods of detection than were available decades ago. But we have vivid memories of the devastation such natural disasters can bring. On March 11, 2011, a 9.0 earthquake off the coast of Japan triggered a deadly twenty-three-foot tsunami in the country's north. The giant waves deluged cities and rural areas alike, sweeping away cars, homes, buildings, a train, and boats, leaving a path of death and devastation in its wake. Video footage showed cars racing away from surging waves. As of June 2011, tens of thousands of people were still in temporary shelters and over 24,000 were confirmed dead or missing.[2]

Yet the earthquakes during the great tribulation will be global in nature, and more powerful than anything this world has yet to experience. Tsunamis and devastating earthquakes will strike in a much wider area, ending the lives of many during this time of

OF COURSE PERSECUTION EXISTS TODAY, ESPECIALLY AGAINST CHRISTIANS. IT WILL BE THE *LEVEL* OF PERSECUTION THAT WILL BE NEW.

judgment. Even so, Jesus called these signs only the beginning. "All these are the beginning of birth pains" (v. 8). The worst is yet to come.

INTENSIFIED PERSECUTION

The fifth sign will be persecution. Of course persecution exists today, especially against Christians. Currently, missionary activity is officially illegal in over fifty nations, which represent approximately one out of every four countries on the planet. It will be the *level* of persecution that will be new, and the target will be especially Jewish believers who have come to Christ since the rapture. Jesus predicts "Then you will be handed over to be persecuted and put to death, and you will be hated by all nations because of me" (v. 9).

Jesus continues, "At that time many will turn away from the faith and will betray and hate each other, and many false prophets will appear and deceive many people. Because of the increase of wickedness, the love of most will grow cold, but he who stands firm to the end will be saved" (vv. 10–13). The expression, "he who stands firm to the end will be saved" has nothing to do with what is generally called "eternal security." What Jesus is saying is that the person who endures to the end of the tribulation period, after so many millions die, will be rescued by Jesus, and will be given the opportunity of entering into the prophesied kingdom. When Jesus speaks of enduring to the end of the age, He has in mind the end of the tribulation period.

THE WORLD IS EVANGELIZED

And then yet, we are surprised by another sign. "And this gospel of the kingdom will be preached in the whole world as a testimony to all nations, and then the end will come" (v. 14). At this point, we must catch our breath and ask: who is preaching this "gospel of the kingdom"? The church has been taken away in the rapture; the special work of the Holy Spirit that came into focus when the church was born on the day of Pentecost has now been removed. Yes, of course the Holy Spirit is still in the world, but in the Old Testament sense of the word.

AGAINST ALL ODDS—THERE ARE PEOPLE BEING SAVED DURING THE TRIBULATION PERIOD.

Antichrist is beginning to mobilize and has signed a peace covenant with Israel, and yet—against all odds—there are people being saved during the tribulation period. Who are these people, and who preached the gospel of the kingdom to them?

Perhaps a clue is found in Revelation chapter 7, where we have John's vision of the 144,000 saints sealed by God.

> After this I saw four angels standing at the four corners of the earth, holding back the four winds of the earth to prevent any wind from blowing on the land or on the sea or on any tree. Then I saw another angel coming up from the east, having the seal of the living God. He called out in a loud voice to the four angels who had been given power to harm the land and the sea: "Do not harm the land or the sea or the trees until we put a seal on the foreheads of the servants of our God. "Then I heard the number of those who were sealed: 144,000 from all the tribes of Israel." (vv. 1–4)

Apparently God is saying, "I am going to restrain My wrath while 144,000 Jews are sealed so that they might not be killed during the tribulation." Those scholars who believe that God has no future program for Israel teach that this special group of individuals must be the church. Yet the 144,000 are identified as the twelve tribes of Israel. So if we take this passage with any degree of literalness, we have to believe that this group is indeed very Jewish. This is not the church, but rather a reference to a future remnant of Israel that God is going to use during the tribulation period.

How are these Jews converted, if in fact the church has already been raptured to heaven? There will be no Christian evangelists available immediately after the church has been taken to heaven. Perhaps this special group will be converted in a dramatic fashion, something like Paul was on his way to Damascus. The disappearance of the Christians at the rapture could be the impetus for many to investigate the gospel by reading the Bible or listening to messages preached by Christian ministers available on CD or as podcasts. God may simply work in their hearts and show them that Christ is their Messiah. They will be encouraged to believe on Jesus and they will respond.

God can use whatever means He wishes to communicate the gospel. Obviously, in this era He is committed to using us, the church, to get the gospel to the whole world as Jesus admonishes us to do. However, He can if He wishes use an angel to proclaim the message. In fact, the book of Revelation teaches just that.

Listen to these words from Revelation 14:6–7:

> Then I saw another angel flying in midair, and he had the eternal gospel to proclaim to those who live on the earth—to every nation, tribe, language and people. He said in a loud voice, "Fear God and give him glory, because the hour of his judgment has come. Worship him who made the heavens, the earth, the sea and the springs of water."

Tragically, we as a church have failed to get the gospel to the whole world. There are many Christians in all the various countries of the world, but there are also many countries, particularly in the Islamic world, where the number of Christians is very small. If God wants to reach them with an angel during the tribulation period, He can do as He wishes. Imagine an angel flying over a nation, say the United States, and proclaiming with a loud voice, "This is the gospel." Is it any wonder that many will believe?

THE ANTICHRIST VISITS JERUSALEM

At this point, we will add other pieces to the prophecy puzzle that I hope will help us understand the possible sequence of events that will take place during the tribulation period. We must listen again to the words of Jesus: "So when you see standing in the holy place 'the abomination that causes desolation,' spoken of through the prophet Daniel—let the reader understand—then let those who are in Judea flee to the mountains" (Matthew 24: 15–16). Here again we encounter the "abomination of desolation" which we have already explained in the previous chapter. As we pointed out, there is reason to believe that Antichrist will make a covenant with Israel that apparently guarantees the nation's peace. (Daniel 9:27). People will think, "At last we have someone who can step into the Middle East and who can say to Israel, 'War is over because I have enough power to guarantee your existence.'" During that period of time there will be a time of relative peace in the Middle East and, for that matter, the world. The Antichrist's rule will bring stability to all nations.

Imagine the temple in Jerusalem rebuilt. This will certainly take a miraculous work of God. The twenty-acre plot of land in Jerusalem where the Jewish temples once stood is occupied by the impressive Muslim Dome of the Rock, a historic Islamic mosque. There would hardly be enough space available to build a temple next to it; and of course tearing down the huge Dome would enrage the world. References to the rebuilt temple include Christ's prediction here in Matthew 24, but also 2 Thessalonians 2:4 and Revelation 11:1–3.

If the signing of a covenant begins the tribulation period and brings about a period of peace that even enables the temple to be rebuilt, that stability will be shattered three and one-half years later when Antichrist pays a special visit to Jerusalem. This deceptive and evil man shows his true colors when he goes into the

PEOPLE ALL OVER THE WORLD WILL SAY TO THEMSELVES, "LOOK AT THE MIRACLE THIS ANTICHRIST HAS DONE."

temple and proclaims himself to be God (2 Thessalonians 2:5–12).

As we have learned, an image will be set up in the temple that everybody is supposed to worship. It appears to be a living image, an image that comes to life, and people all over the world will say to themselves, "Look at the miracle this Antichrist has done," and they will worship both the Beast (Antichrist) and the image. And that is what Jesus called, "the abomination of desolation."

This will be the ultimate insult to God. For a brief period, Satan has what he's always wanted, namely the opportunity to duplicate God and attract the admiration and worship of many millions of people throughout the world. Some will not worship him, but many will. So that is what Jesus meant when He spoke of the "abomination of desolation in the holy place." This will be the ultimate sacrilege.

THE PERSECUTION OF THE JEWS

Jesus continues by describing what will happen to the Jewish people during this horrible time:

> Then let those who are in Judea flee to the mountains. Let no one on the roof of his house go down to take anything out of the house. Let no one in the field go back to get his cloak. How dreadful it will be in those days for pregnant women and nursing mothers! Pray that your flight will not take place in winter or on the Sabbath. For then there will be great distress, unequaled from the beginning of the world until now—and never to be equaled again. (Matthew 24:16–21)

When the Antichrist proclaims himself as God, Jerusalem will immediately be ground zero of the holocaust. Antichrist will begin to round up Jews to destroy them, fulfilling Hitler's evil vision. When the Antichrist begins his persecutions, many will take the advice of Jesus and flee as quickly as possible. They will not even have enough time to take clothes with them nor able to bring enough food in their satchels. Jesus said they should pray that their flight not be in winter or on the Sabbath. Since the Jewish people believe they should not travel on the Sabbath, there will be a great deal of hindrance for those who want to flee the city.

And how will they stay alive in the mountains? In Revelation, Israel is likened unto a woman who flees to the mountains and is taken care of by God, where she is guarded and fed. The nation will be protected in the wilderness for three and one-half years (Revelation 12:13–14).

Where will they flee to live? We're not told exactly, but if you have seen the film *Indiana Jones and the Last Crusade*, you are familiar with a tunnel that leads to the ancient city of Petra. In fact, some of us had the privilege of visiting Petra recently, and visualized what it might look like if the Jews fled Jerusalem to live there.

Meanwhile, the judgments of the book of Revelation begin to unravel on the earth. Jesus says clearly that there will be tribulation as has never been since in the history of the world. "If those days had not been cut short, no one would survive" (Matthew 24:22). But as predicted, some will survive to populate the coming millennial kingdom.

Then Jesus continues:

> At that time if anyone says to you, "Look, here is the Christ!" or, "There he is!" do not believe it. For false Christs and false prophets will appear and perform great signs and miracles to deceive even the elect—if that were possible. See, I have told you ahead of time. (vv. 23–25)

Jesus returns to the topic of false Christs because now that Antichrist has proclaimed himself to be God, he will have all kinds of emissaries combing the country and singing their dictator's praises. They will encourage everyone to worship him and his image. Jesus warns, despite their claims, "Don't believe them."

THE GLORIOUS RETURN

Now Jesus makes it very clear that when He returns to earth, there will be no question about who He is. No need to convince anyone that He is the Christ. Just read the description of what is to follow:

> For as lightning that comes from the east is visible even in the west, so will be the coming of the Son of Man. Wherever there is a carcass, there the vultures will gather.
>
> Immediately after the distress of those days
>
> "the sun will be darkened,
>   and the moon will not give its light;
> the stars will fall from the sky,
>   and the heavenly bodies will be shaken."
>
> At that time the sign of the Son of Man will appear in the sky, and all the nations of the earth will mourn. They will see the Son of Man coming on the clouds of the sky, with power and great glory. And he will send his angels with a loud trumpet call, and they will gather his elect from the four winds, from one end of the heavens to the other. (vv. 27–31)

Four winds means north, east, south, and west—from all the different areas of the world the angels seek and find God's elect. Jesus has returned to end the fighting and dictatorship of the Antichrist. Also, those believers who survived the tribulation will be judged and allowed entrance into the kingdom that Jesus is about to establish.

Because this event is so momentous we discuss it in detail in chapter 7.

PONDERING THE FUTURE

What do we make of all of this? Let's take a moment to think about what the suffering of the tribulation should reveal to us about God and His purposes.

First, consider the severity of God's wrath and His anger against sin! Even in evangelical circles today there is a growing belief that we should just emphasize the positive aspects of Christianity—how Jesus can make you a better husband, a better mother, a better business leader. Of course we agree that God cares about these areas of life, but solely focusing on the more acceptable attributes of God domesticates Him. We often make God into our own image. We have made a God that we can live with who doesn't like sin, but tolerates it indefinitely. We have made God into someone who is very happy with the way we are. The great tribulation exposes this lie.

Jonathan Edwards is frequently criticized for his sermon "Sinners in the Hands of an Angry God." Yet what he says about God, hell, and the gospel are very true to Scripture. It is just that our generation has remade God to be more to our liking. And the "designer Jesus" of our culture is not the Jesus of the Scriptures.

> EVEN IN EVANGELICAL CIRCLES TODAY THERE IS A GROWING BELIEF THAT WE SHOULD JUST EMPHASIZE THE POSITIVE ASPECTS OF CHRISTIANITY.

Fact is, we have no idea how offensive our sin is to God. The reason that the gospel is so wonderful is because Jesus bore the wrath of God for us. Whether in the Old Testament or the New, sin always elicits the wrath of God. And in the future, God's full fury against sin will be demonstrated. Again we quote Jesus, "For then there will be great distress, unequaled from the beginning of the world until now—and never to be equaled again" (v. 21). What a frightful future!

The second lesson is that there is always a great separation when God's judgment strikes. The glorious return of Jesus ends the great tribulation, but then a judgment must take place to determine who can enter the newly established millennial kingdom. The sheep are welcomed into the kingdom—and as for the goats, they go into everlasting fire. No one is in the middle: you are either a sheep or you are a goat; either you have come to trust Jesus as Messiah, or you haven't. This is one of many great divides in the Bible—the great separation. "Then they will go away to eternal punishment, but the righteous to eternal life" (Matthew 25:46).

During the early days when farmers feared that a prairie fire might consume their homes, they thought of a way to make sure that if such a fire began it would not come to their buildings. On a day when the wind was favorable, they would begin a controlled fire that would burn the surrounding area. If a prairie fire came in their direction, they knew it would stop at the place where the fire had already been.

We are warned that it is a fearful thing to fall into the hands of the living God, for our God is a consuming fire (Hebrews 10:31). Read the book of Revelation and you will see how fearful it really is to come under God's judgment. But when we trust Christ, we are standing where the fire of God's wrath has already burned. We are in effect, standing where the fire of God's wrath has already been. If not, we will be thrown into the lake of fire.

In the next chapter we will turn our attention to the first three and one-half years of the tribulation when the world will believe that peace has arrived in the Middle East, and for that matter, in the rest of the world. A number of countries will attempt to capitalize on Israel's vulnerability and organize to invade the land. But they will soon discover that God sides with Israel in this conflict and their judgment will be swift and total. God will personally destroy them without Israel firing a single shot.

To that event we now turn.

NOTES

1. Based on the latest 2011 statistics from http://dreamer.me/world-hunger.

2. "Tsunami in Japan: 2011." Accessed at http://www.infoplease.com/science/weather/japan-tsunami-2011.html.

CHAPTER SIX

THE KING
DESTROYS NATIONS

*A careful examination of Scripture reveals a
number of different ways that God has dealt with tyrants
who curse the Jewish people throughout history.
But Ezekiel warns us that certain leaders of certain nations
will face an unprecedented and cataclysmic judgment in the
last days. That is what the War of Gog and Magog is all about,
and it may be here sooner than most people think.*
—Joel Rosenberg

No religion is as hostile to Christianity as Islam. The Muslim religion not only denies the deity of Christ but even asserts that He was not crucified but was taken directly to heaven. Thus the heart of the Christian gospel—that Jesus Christ died for our sins and rose again—is vehemently denied. In recent decades a radical form of Islam has emerged that instigates persecutions, threats and other means of torture against Christian churches, individuals, and institutions. Islam's schemes to rule the world are based on its authoritative books such as the Qur'an and the Hadith.

Certainly the majority of Muslims are not in favor of terrorism or extending Islamic influence by force. Many have become westernized; others point to the more tolerant passages of the Qur'an to define their lifestyles and attitudes. God has brought many Muslims to the United States where we have the privilege of befriending them and also introducing them to the Gospel of Christ. We must welcome them as neighbors.

However, particularly in the Middle East, Islam's hatred for the Jews is even more intense than its hatred for Christians. Three times in the Qur'an the Jews are referred to as "pigs and apes" (7:166; 2:65; 5:60). Muhammad's hatred for the Jews not only has found expression in the Qur'an but has been the legacy of the Muslim faith throughout its history. Perhaps the most telling picture of warfare against the Jews is found in the Hadith, the sayings of Muhammad: "The last hour will not come until the Muslims fight against the Jews and the Muslims kill them, until the Jews hide themselves, and the stones and the trees would speak up saying, 'There is a Jew hiding behind me, come and kill him'" (The Hadith, Sahi Muslim, Book 40#6985). Given this irrational rage against the Jews, we should not be surprised that the Bible predicts that a number of Muslim countries will join a powerful ally to launch a massive assault against Israel, only to be severely judged and annihilated by God Himself.

> I BELIEVE GOD WILL INTERVENE TO SPARE THIS LAND SO THAT ALL OF HIS PROMISES TO THE JEWISH PEOPLE CAN STILL BE FULFILLED.

We can confidently predict that the notion of a "two-state solution" to the Middle East crisis (a Palestinian state and an Israeli state coexisting side by side) is impossible. Palestinian leaders have proven that they are not as much interested in territory as they are in Jewish blood. Radicalized groups would use any such two-state developments only to gain a stronger foothold to eventually "push Israel into the sea."

IN THE END TIMES, THE UNITED STATES WILL HAVE NO INFLUENCE WHEN THE FINAL CHAPTERS OF WORLD HISTORY ARE WRITTEN.

Of course there has been suffering and injustice on both sides in this ongoing dispute; many innocent Palestinians have been displaced and deprived of basic rights. But despite international pressure for Israel to submit to increasingly unreasonable Palestinian demands, I believe God will intervene to spare this land so that all of His promises to the Jewish people can still be fulfilled. But we are ahead of the story.

WHAT ABOUT THE UNITED STATES?

There is nothing we can do to halt the fact of the eventual demise of the United States. Perhaps we can postpone our nation's downfall through our witness to the gospel, our continual efforts to maintain our freedoms and by electing government officials who are willing to defend our country, protect our freedoms, and do what they can to elevate our moral climate. But in the end times, the United States will have no influence when the final chapters of world history are written. As for Chicago, Los Angeles, and New York, these cities, along with the others in the world, will eventually be destroyed. Speaking of a future Babylon we read, "The great city split into three parts, *and the cities of the nations collapsed.* God remembered Babylon the Great and gave her the cup filled with the wine of the fury of his wrath" (Revelation 16:19, italics added). There is debate as to whether this is a reference to a future city of Babylon yet to be built, or whether Babylon stands for the collective evil of the cities of the world. Either way, we find that eventually in the fury of God's wrath, *the cities of the nations will collapse.*

Not only is there no mention of the United States in end-time events, but when the Scriptures predict that Antichrist will rule the world, that obviously would include his rule over America. All nations, at the pain of death, will have surrendered their independence to the one-world government and one-world religion. The United States will also have submitted itself to this global regime headed by Antichrist.

Perhaps one reason the United States will not figure in the events of the last days is that the pretribulation rapture will have caused the disappearance of Christians, and without their influence and numbers, the nation will be impoverished morally and economically. Many non-Christians will be glad we're gone, but with millions having left their jobs without warning, and speculation rampant as to how these strange events can be explained, the nation will find itself teetering on the edge of confusion and internal self-destruction.

Our oil crisis might play a part in the demise of this great nation. After all, we desperately need foreign oil and it could be that as the years progress, the United States will begin to ally itself more closely with oil-rich Arab states than it does with Israel. Even in recent years, it is evident that our nation's support of Israel is in decline. For example, when some politicians suggest that Israel should retreat to her pre-1967 borders, which would render her hopelessly vulnerable to Palestinian attacks, we know that the United States is no longer the ally it once was.

A third reason could be terrorism. Whether through military force, cyber attacks, biological warfare, or some other form of brute force, the potential for massive deaths and destruction is very real. Because we are so interdependent, a serious attack in one part of the country could cripple the whole nation. A nation filled with fear would withdraw into a survival mode with mobs roaming the streets in search of food and destroying the infrastructure.

Regardless of what triggers it, there will be a financial collapse spurred on by those who hate "Wall Street" and believe that capitalism must be destroyed to bring about "equality." We just have to look to the recent histories of Russia, China, and Eastern Europe to see what happens when a government seizes control "in the best interests of all the people." In place of democracy and freedom, brutal government controls will be imposed on fearful citizens. Given that the economies of the world are so closely attuned to one another, we can expect that an economic meltdown would paralyze the Western world. If the United States suffers a terrorist attack along with an economic disaster, the results on a human level would be catastrophic.

Without the United States protecting Israel, we can understand that some nations will take advantage of Antichrist's peace treaty and seek to attack this tiny country. At last, they think, they will finally destroy Israel and kill the Jews to fulfill Muhammad's prediction. In the end, this coalition will be destroyed, not by Israel or the United States but by God alone. The God who through His prophet predicted these terrifying events is the same God who will in the end destroy the invading armies.

THE REBIRTH OF ISRAEL

Before I describe the nations that form this coalition, we should remind ourselves that God predicted that Israel would be revived as a nation. Almost certainly, Ezekiel's vision of dry bones is being fulfilled before our eyes. Ezekiel 37:1–5 reads:

> The hand of the Lord was upon me, and he brought me out by the Spirit of the Lord and set me in the middle of a valley; it was full of bones. He led me back and forth among them, and I saw a great many bones on the floor of the valley, bones that were very dry. He asked me, "Son of man, can these bones live?"

I said, "O Sovereign Lord, you alone know."

Then he said to me, "Prophesy to these bones and say to them, 'Dry bones, hear the word of the Lord! This is what the Sovereign Lord says to these bones: I will make breath enter you, and you will come to life.'"

As Ezekiel prophesied over the bones, sinews begin to come together, and the bones begin to connect. Eventually, these bones come to life. Fortunately, it's not up to us to figure out the mystery of what Ezekiel saw. God Himself gives us the interpretation: The Lord says in verses 11–14:

> Then he said to me: "Son of man, these bones are the whole house of Israel. They say, 'Our bones are dried up and our hope is gone; we are cut off.' Therefore prophesy and say to them: 'This is what the Sovereign Lord says: O my people, I am going to open your graves and bring you up from them; I will bring you back to the land of Israel. Then you, my people, will know that I am the Lord, when I open your graves and bring you up from them. I will put my Spirit in you and you will live, and I will settle you in your own land. Then you will know that I the Lord have spoken, and I have done it, declares the Lord.'"

When Israel was formed as a nation in 1948, the bones started to come together, but today the bones are still dry; by that I mean that the nation lacks spiritual life. Officially and unofficially, Israel does not recognize Jesus Christ as the Messiah. Sad to say, many Jewish people have left their faith and have become agnostics or even atheists. They are skeptical of (or outright disbelieve) their own Old Testament Scriptures.

Evangelicals who uncritically side with Israel because they are "chosen of God" must keep in mind that the present nation exists in unbelief. Because of our love of the gospel, we must also gladly show loyalty and friendship to our Palestinian brothers and sisters who daily suffer for their faith in the face of Islam and also because of the restrictions Israel has had to impose in these regions in order to fight terrorism. Yet a day is coming when the Jewish nation will turn from unbelief to God and accept Jesus as Messiah. God says, in effect, "I am going to give you life, and I will even put My Spirit within you." Later on in this chapter, God says He will cleanse His people and give them a new heart. (vv. 21–23). Yes, eventually, when Jesus Christ returns, the Jewish people in existence at that time will come to believe in Him.

THE COMING CONFLICT

Ezekiel 38 and 39 describe an amazing six-nation invasion of Israel—or, I should say, an amazing *attempt* to invade Israel. First, we should note that this event has never happened before; never in history has this coalition been formed, nor has such a group of nations gathered with the intention of destroying Israel and taking her wealth. Second, it is important to realize that this will happen "in the latter days." So we are wise to locate this event in the sequence of end-time prophecy.

But when will this invasion occur? Some biblical scholars think that it will happen in our day, before the rapture of the church. However, it seems best to place these events in the first half of the great tribulation period for two reasons. One, as we shall see, this takes place at a time when Israel feels secure during a time of peace. As far as we know, only when Antichrist signs his peace treaty will there be a period of peace that would make Israel vulnerable to an invasion. Then, the direct judgment of God on this coalition fits best during the tribulation period when the wrath of God is poured out on the world. Certainly in world history, there has never been a time when nations have been destroyed directly by God without the use of any countermilitary force.

THE COALITION FORMS

Ezekiel begins his prophecy by saying, "The word of the Lord came to me." Just think: this prophet has a direct word from God, receiving information not from the intelligence community, but from the God of the Universe who not only knows the future but planned it! Ezekiel, of all people, was able to read the headlines of the distant future. He had the ultimate inside information.

Let's read Ezekiel 38:1–6:

> The word of the Lord came to me: "Son of man, set your face against Gog, of the land of Magog, the chief prince of Meshech and Tubal; prophesy against him and say: 'This is what the Sovereign Lord says: I am against you, O Gog, chief prince of Meshech and Tubal. I will turn you around, put hooks in your jaws and bring you out with your whole army—your horses, your horsemen fully armed, and a great horde with large and small shields, all of them brandishing their swords. Persia, Cush and Put will be with them, all with shields and helmets, also Gomer with all its troops, and Beth Togarmah from the far north with all its troops—the many nations with you.'"

We're not readily acquainted with these ancient names, but they have their contemporary counterparts. Many scholars have connected these countries with the table of nations in the book of Genesis, and have given us an interpretation which I believe is reasonably accurate.

Let's try to unpack these names and their descriptions.

Gog is the word for ruler, and *Magog* apparently refers to Russia and perhaps those countries that are south of Russia, countries that were a part of the former Soviet Union. There are reasons as to why we believe that Magog might be a reference to Russia. God says, "I'm going to bring you out from the far north" (see vv. 6, 15). Then in the next chapter we again are reminded that the coalition begins in "the far north" (39:2) or even better, "the uttermost part of the north." If you put your finger on a map of Jerusalem and go straight toward the North Pole, you will pass through Russia; in fact, your finger will pass over Moscow.

Also, Jerome, a prominent leader of the early church, indicated that Magog was located north of the Caucasus Mountains near the Caspian Sea. And even a few centuries before Jerome, the historian Josephus, who was a contemporary of Christ, associated the name with the Scythians who lived near the Black Sea, in the southern part of modern Russia.[1] So this would include the "Stans" of today: Kazakhstan, Kyrgyzstan, Uzbekistan, Turkmenistan, and Tajikistan. Perhaps also Afghanistan could be part of the territory.[2]

Recently my wife and I visited St. Petersburg, Russia, where I spoke at a seminary and preached in a church. We met many fine Christian friends. These dear brothers and sisters have suffered greatly under the Soviet Union and even now live with varying degrees of government hostility and economic restrictions. It would be wrong for us to categorize Russia (the Bear) as consisting only of people making up an evil empire who have designs to join with Muslim forces to go against Israel. Believers in Christ will already have been raptured before these events occur, and if even if these dear saints were alive during this battle, they almost certainly would have no part in the evil schemed to destroy Israel. Nor should we paint the Muslim nations with a broad brush; when we speak about nations, we do not necessarily mean every citizen of that nation will agree with the evil intent of their leaders.

WHEN WE SPEAK ABOUT NATIONS, WE DO NOT NECESSARILY MEAN EVERY CITIZEN OF THAT NATION WILL AGREE WITH THE EVIL INTENT OF THEIR LEADERS.

However, I must say that the present Russian rulers are supportive of the Muslim countries that surround their borders, and it is easy to see how Russia will be tempted to join a Muslim alliance in its effort to shift the balance of power away from the West. Perhaps in our day we can already see political alliances moving toward a coalition that will be aligned against Israel. We already know that Russia has in the past worked with Islamic nations, supplying Syria and Egypt with military weapons to be used in their wars against Israel. And, more recently, Russia has supplied weapons to Hezbollah in Lebanon and to Hamas in Gaza to aid these countries in their fight against Israel. More significant is that Russia has helped Iran develop weapons, including selling a nuclear power plant to that nation.[3]

Also, and this is a frightening scenario, Russia itself is vulnerable to becoming a Muslim nation within a few decades. The demographics show that while Russian families are small (often due to high abortion rates), the Muslim population is growing exponentially. In 1991 there were 300 mosques in Russia, and by 2006 there were approximately 8,000. It is estimated that by 2015, Russia will have about 25,000 mosques. So if Russia becomes an Islamic nation, it will identify even more closely with other Muslim nations in their common desire to destroy Israel.

Next, Ezekiel mentions the names Meshech and Tubal, which are best identified with the regions within and around Turkey. And two other names, Gomer and Beth Togarmah, refer to various countries that border Turkey. If these identifications are correct, we can expect that in the days ahead Russia will have closer ties with Turkey, a country that prides itself in its secularism, but is moving toward a more Islamic fundamentalist government.

Other countries that are listed as a part of this alliance include Persia, which is modern-day Iran, whose current prime minister Ahmadinejad has denied the Holocaust and has been frequently quoted as saying he plans to wipe Israel off the map. Isn't it intriguing that Russia has trained more than a thousand Iranian nuclear scientists? Russia says that it is willing to defend

Iran, which makes Iran's pursuit of nuclear weapons even more critical in the days ahead.

Next is Cush, an African nation that should not be identified as modern-day Ethiopia but rather the Sudan. So, please keep in mind that the Cush of Ezekiel's day is what we call the Sudan today, a region that has recently been divided into Northern and Southern Sudan.

The next nation listed is Put, which today is Libya. In October of 2011 the assassination of Muammar Gaddafi marked another victory for the so-called "Arab Spring," a reference to a revolutionary wave of demonstrations, protests, and fighting that has shaken the Arab world. Regimes have been toppled in Tunisia, Egypt, and now Libya. But even before Gaddafi's body had been buried, the transitional leader called for Libya to become a Muslim state with Sharia law, the rule of the land. Once again the radicals are insisting that there be a "Purer Islam" in these countries; thus sadly, the so-called "Arab Spring" of 2011 is beginning to look much like an "Islamic winter."

You should be wondering, "If the invaders are coming from the north, how can these two African countries participate in the invasion?" Perhaps to avoid going through Egypt (there is evidence that this nation will be under the control of Antichrist), they will transport their troops by boat to the "northern regions" of the Mediterranean and there join the lead nations in their journey toward Israel.

Where is Saudi Arabia in this lineup? We'd expect this Islamic nation to be front and center in the proposed invasion of Israel. Many scholars believe that Sheba and Dedan (v. 13) are a reference to Saudi Arabia. However, if this is a reference to Saudi Arabia, these nations evidently do not join the coalition but simply offer a mild protest to the invasion. "Have you come to plunder? Have you gathered your hordes to loot, to carry off silver and gold, to take away livestock and goods and to seize much plunder?" (v. 13). Saudi Arabia, though a Muslim country, has often served as a Western ally or friend, so it is possible that it will join the Western coalition that will be under the heel of the Antichrist. Or perhaps the nation has already been destroyed in a previous battle.

Virtually all the nations led by Russia are entirely Islamic. This religion that has consistently fought against Christ and His people will now unite to destroy the Jews, their most hated enemy. But it will not turn out as planned. Their evil designs will come to naught.

THE REASONS FOR THE INVASION

Why will these nations gather in battle against Israel? We are told, they are coming "to plunder and loot . . . against the re-settled ruins and the people gathered from the nations" (v. 12) Perhaps they are invading because Israel will have found a way to greatly benefit from the minerals found in the Dead Sea; or perhaps the "spoil" not only includes the taking the riches of the land, but also to capture the city of Jerusalem that Muslims have always hoped to conquer for themselves. No doubt their larger plan is to crush Israel, to capture its wealth and resettle in the land and turn it once again into an Islamic nation.

According to this account, they will not be using nuclear weapons, and understandably so. To use a nuclear weapon against Israel would be not only to destroy the country (including the Islamic holy sites) but also to risk casualties and injury to their own people. The armies are described as riding on horses (v. 15). This prophecy, was of course written, in the language that Ezekiel would have understood. Such references might be symbolic, but what is clear is that this group of armies has come together with millions of soldiers to invade Israel. They want to destroy the Jews whom they have been taught to hate through-out the centuries. And they expect to do their ghastly deed with overwhelming force.

As already indicated, this invasion will take place during a time when Israel is at peace, "You will say, 'I will invade a land of unwalled villages; I will attack a peaceful and unsuspecting people—all of them living without walls and without gates and bars'" (v. 11). This will take place at a time when Israel is not on high alert. Evidently, confident that the mighty ruler of Europe (Antichrist) will protect them, they do not fear the invasion. Only Antichrist's peace treaty could create such confidence.

THE ANNIHILATION OF THE COALITION

Regardless of the particular timeline, it is important that we focus on what the text itself emphasizes. These Islamic nations that are dedicated to the destruction of Israel will now experience their most humiliating defeat—or, more accurately, obliteration.

Verses 15–18 tell us:

> You will come from your place in the far north, you and many nations with you, all of them riding on horses, a great horde, a mighty army. You will advance against my people Israel like a cloud that covers the land. In days to come, O Gog, I will bring you against my land, so that the nations may know me when I show myself holy through you before their eyes. "This is what the Sovereign Lord says: Are you not the one I spoke of in former days by my servants the prophets of Israel? At that time they prophesied for years that I would bring you against them. This is what will happen in that day: When Gog attacks the land of Israel, my hot anger will be aroused, declares the Sovereign Lord."

God is not finished yet. Yes, He will display His holiness against these nations that have come to destroy His people. Read this description of how the battle will end:

In anger the Lord says,

> I will summon a sword against Gog on all my mountains, declares the Sovereign Lord. Every man's sword will be against his brother. I will execute judgment upon him with plague and bloodshed; I will pour down torrents of rain, hailstones and burning sulfur on him and on his troops and on the many nations with him. And so I will show my greatness and my holiness, and I will make myself known in the sight of many nations. Then they will know that I am the Lord." (vv. 21–23)

Initially God will send an earthquake; then in the confusion, the enemies of Israel will begin to kill one another. Following this will come rain, hailstones, fire, and sulfur. In the next chapter we are told that it will take seven months to bury the dead (39:12). In fact, a whole valley will be filled with dead bodies, and it would take even longer than seven months were it not for the fact that the birds of the air come and eat the carcasses of the dead. What a powerful judgment.

One puzzling aspect of this description is this prediction, "Then those who live in the towns of Israel will go out and use the weapons for fuel and burn them up—the small and large shields, the bows and arrows, the war clubs and spears. For seven years they will use them for fuel. They will not need to gather wood from the fields or cut it from the forests, because they will use the weapons for fuel" (39:9–10). A seven-year period would stretch into the millennial kingdom.

IT IS UNLIKELY GOD WOULD HAVE REVEALED TO EZEKIEL JET PLANES, MISSILES, AND TANKS.

Again we are faced with questions: Are they really going to fight this battle with clubs and spears? Where are the missiles and tanks? Some have suggested that perhaps the armies will have to revert to primitive methods of warfare because all of the modern methods of warfare may be paralyzed by huge infrastructure and cyberattacks. The other possibility is that Ezekiel was seeing this in ways that were understandable to him over 2,500 years ago, and meaningful to his own people. It is unlikely God would have revealed to Ezekiel jet planes, missiles, and tanks. Perhaps the weapons used for fuel are actually unexploded bombs containing uranium and titanium.

Truth is, we don't know how to translate ancient imagery into modern equivalents. But what is clear is that God is describing a battle that has not yet happened; a battle that names countries, describes mountains, and predicts a massive victory to the glory of God. And this victory will prove once again God's faithfulness to the Jewish people and His determination to protect "His land."

Islam has set its face against the God of the Bible; it has rejected Jesus, God's Son and it has vehemently schemed to "push Israel into the sea," but God has intervened. "I will display my glory among the nations, and all the nations will see the punishment I inflict and the hand I lay upon them. From that day forward the house of Israel will know that I am the Lord their God" (39:21–22).

Let's take a moment to speculate. If this battle takes place during the first three and one-half years of the tribulation, we can certainly understand that the balance of power would shift and Antichrist would basically be free of any competition. With Russia and its Islamic allies destroyed, Antichrist could bask in the glory of worldwide triumph. And with the weakening, if not destruction of the Islamic powers, he would be free to rebuild the temple in Jerusalem to please the Jews and to plan his own spectacular claim to be God. Individual Muslims would object, but there would be no Islamic nation capable of launching an attack.

IMPLICATIONS FOR TODAY

What do we learn from the defeat of this coalition of Israel's enemies? First, it is a powerful reminder of the sovereignty of God. Who brings these nations down from the north to attack Israel? God says He Himself will do this: "I will turn you around, put hooks in your jaws and bring you out with your whole army" (38:4). God is able to so work in the hearts of people (even in the hearts of his enemies) that they will voluntarily do what He wants them to do. In other words, God is able to direct the nations in such a way that they do His bidding even though they are still responsible for their actions.

FIGURATIVELY SPEAKING, GOD CAN TAKE A BRUSH AND SWEEP THE DUST INTO HIS BUCKET WHENEVER HE WISHES TO.

God will have tolerated these nations' hatred for Israel long enough. God is patient, but there comes a time when a nation's cup of iniquity is full. These nations that have so long defied Him will unite against Israel according to God's timetable. When they are ripe for judgment, they will fall into His hands.

Isaiah said, "The nations are like a drop in a bucket; they are regarded as dust on the scales" (40:15). Figuratively speaking, God can take a brush and sweep the dust into His bucket whenever He wishes. Even when nations are in the hands of Satan and do his bidding, they are still ultimately in God's hand and must do *His* bidding. God uses Satan and overrides the schemes of the evil one according to His plan and purpose.

Second, this invasion and subsequent judgment reveals the terror of God. The chapter opens with the declaration, "I am against you, O Gog" and ends with a dreadful judgment against this coalition. The judgment is so severe it might offend our sensibilities. However, when we read the book of Revelation we see similar judgments; horrific battles, unimaginable natural disasters with starvation, and human suffering that rivals the Holocaust. We shall discover that Jesus Himself returns to earth with flaming fire, taking vengeance on those who do not know God (2 Thessalonians 1:8–9).

HERE WE SEE THE SOVEREIGNTY OF GOD AND THE TERROR OF GOD, BUT WE ALSO SEE THE MERCY OF GOD.

We treasure the grace of God, but we should also revere the terror of God, which is just as much an aspect of His character and attributes. And He will vindicate His honor: "I will make known my holy name among my people Israel. I will no longer let my holy name be profaned" (Ezekiel 39:7). The patience of God will eventually come to an end.

Yes, here we see the sovereignty of God, and the terror of God, but we also see the mercy of God. In the countries that are a part of this coalition there are presently many fine believers, and their place in heaven is secured. Such believers will, of course, be raptured to meet Christ in the air; and those who trust Christ after the rapture will be members of that great throng that "no one could count" (Revelation 7:9) "who have come out of the great tribulation; they have washed their robes and made them white in the blood of the Lamb" (v. 14). Those who are left behind but come to faith in Christ will live to populate the millennial kingdom. Either way, their souls will be saved and their bodies resurrected according to God's timetable. They shall live forever in God's presence.

Furthermore, God will also show mercy to Israel. God is even now preparing Israel for the great tribulation that will further refine His people and prepare them to accept Jesus Christ as their Messiah. The *judgment* of God will lead many to accept the *grace* of God.

Grace means that we receive a gift we don't deserve; mercy means withholding the judgment we do deserve. In Jesus, we receive both, and rejoice in His salvation.

The story is told of a woman who came to Napoleon and said,

"Would you pardon my son? You have the ability to do it." Napoleon said, "He is not worthy to be pardoned." She said, "I know he isn't worthy, but I am appealing to your mercy," and Napoleon said, "He doesn't deserve mercy." And she accurately answered, "If he deserved mercy he wouldn't need the pardon I seek. I'm asking *for mercy*."

When we ask for mercy, we are asking for what we don't deserve. And yet, because God is merciful He responds to those who admit they need it the most.

Mercy there was great and grace was free.

Pardon there was multiplied for me.

There my burdened soul found liberty at Calvary.

Only the mercy of God can keep us from the wrath of God. Blessed are they who take shelter in Him. They need not fear the coming judgments.

"God is our refuge and strength, an ever-present help in trouble. Therefore we will not fear, though the earth give way and the mountains fall into the heart of the sea. . . . Be still, and know that I am God; I will be exalted among the nations, I will be exalted in the earth" (Psalm 46:1–2, 10).

NOTES

1. Renald Showers, *The Coming Apocalypse: A Study of Replacement Theology vs. God's Faithfulness in the End-Times* (Bellmawr, New Jersey: The Friends of Israel Gospel Ministry, 2009), 93.

2. John F. Walvoord with Mark Hitchcock, *Armageddon, Oil, and Terror* (Wheaton, IL: Tyndale House Publishers, rev. 2007), 89.

3. Showers, 95. Showers gives additional documentation to show Russia's commitment to provide strategic help to Iran and other Muslim nations.

CHAPTER SEVEN

THE KING RETURNS
TO CONQUER

*The Second Coming will proceed as the most
glorious epiphany of all time. . . . As Jesus slowly ascended
up into the cloud, to the glory of the Father in the highest
heaven, just so He will return. When He returns all
will see Him. Only a few saw Him leave.*
—Ronald Allen

We now come to the most spectacular and dramatic event
that we could possibly imagine, an event yet to take place
on Planet Earth. Nothing akin to it has ever happened in the past
and nothing like it will ever happen a second time. I'm speaking
about the glorious return of Jesus Christ back to earth. Since the
rapture of the church will already have taken place years before
this, this event is the second stage of the coming of Jesus. This
time Jesus actually returns to this earth—and His arrival will, in
one way or another, affect the entire population of the globe.

IN THE DRAMATIC EVENT BEFORE US WE WILL SEE NOT ONLY THE LOVE OF JESUS BUT THE METICULOUS JUSTICE OF JESUS.

Some of the events associated with His glorious return will be shocking, especially for those who think of Jesus only in terms of the gospel accounts, when He went about healing the sick, raising the dead, and blessing the poor. In the dramatic event before us, we will see not only the love of Jesus but the meticulous justice of Jesus. We will see Jesus not as Savior, but as Judge. The implications are staggering.

Yes, we might be surprised at the unstoppable tsunami of judgment that will be hurled upon this planet as it is described in the biblical text. We will see Jesus as we have never seen Him before; the whole world will be mesmerized by His appearance and swift justice. Now at last the redeemer of the world will become the judge of the world.

Before we describe the return of Jesus, we must remember that His appearing will awaken the Jewish people to the fact that He is indeed their long-awaited Messiah. When Paul wrote, "And so all Israel will be saved" (Romans 11:26), he was teaching that there will be a remnant of Jews who will believe on their Messiah, Jesus. They will be saved and enter into the millennial kingdom that Jesus will establish. In a previous chapter we quoted the words of the prophet Zechariah, "They will look on me, the one they have pierced" (12:10). Yes, there is a generation of Israelites who will be redeemed by the returning Christ.

THE CONTEXT OF THE GLORIOUS APPEARING

Let's review what will be happening on earth just as Jesus is about to return. Antichrist will be in full, dark bloom; the mark of the beast will force people to worship the Beast if they want to live. Such worship of Antichrist will be worldwide, except of course among those whose names were written in the "Lamb's

Book of Life." Satan, knowing that his time is short, will initiate one more massive assault on the Jews.

The battle of Armageddon will be in full swing when Jesus returns. The Plain of Megiddo, about sixty miles north of Jerusalem, will evidently be the place where the battle will begin; this might be the central location, but of course armies will be spread out over the entire region extending to Jerusalem. In Revelation 16 we read, "Then I saw three evil spirits that looked like frogs; they came out of the mouth of the dragon, out of the mouth of the beast and out of the mouth of the false prophet. They are spirits of demons performing miraculous signs, and they go out to the kings of the whole world, to gather them for the battle on the great day of God Almighty" (vv. 13–14). The unholy trinity consisting of the dragon (Satan), the Beast (who is the Antichrist), and the false prophet (who is the anti–Holy Spirit) will open their mouths, and from their mouths evil spirits will come, and these spirits will be sent throughout the whole earth to gather the armies of the world to Jerusalem.

This unholy trinity will convince the kings of the earth to assemble at Megiddo to once and for all wrest Jerusalem from Jewish control and destroy the Jews once and for all. However, what they do not know is that before their final assault, King Jesus will return to defend His city and His people. And when they see Jesus coming, they will unite to fight against Him, trying to prevent Him from being installed on the throne of David in Jerusalem. This rebellion is predicted in Psalm 2, where the nations rage against God's Son, trying to prevent Him from being officially installed as Israel's King. So, the armies of the world will gather "for the battle on the great day of God Almighty" (16:14). What begins as a dispute about real estate and vengeance against the Jews will become a massive showdown between Satan and Jesus. This final showdown ends badly for

Satan and his followers; in the ensuing battle, King Jesus spectacularly prevails.

THE RETURN TO THE MOUNT OF OLIVES

Let's focus on the three most important passages in the Bible about the glorious return of Jesus. These passages describe the same event, but help us see it from different perspectives.

God gave the prophet Zechariah a graphic and chilling description of the criminal activity that will be happening in Jerusalem just before the glorious descent of Jesus to the Mount of Olives. The treasures of Jerusalem will be plundered; then, more ominously, we read, "I will gather all the nations to Jerusalem to fight against it; the city will be captured, the houses ransacked, and the women raped. Half of the city will go into exile, but the rest of the people will not be taken from the city" (14:2). Warfare will be taking place from house to house as the armies approach Jerusalem. There will be unspeakable crimes, and half the people will go into exile.

This evil invasion of the city will be interrupted by Jesus' return: "Then the Lord will go out and fight against those nations, as he fights in the day of battle. On that day his feet will stand on the Mount of Olives, east of Jerusalem, and the Mount of Olives will be split in two from east to west, forming a great valley, with half of the mountain moving north and half moving south" (vv. 3–4).

Amazing! Jesus will return to the Mount of Olives. How appropriate that His feet shall stand on this famous mountain! About 2,500 years ago, the prophet Ezekiel saw the Shekinah Glory of God leave the temple area and disappear over the Mount of Olives (11:22–23). How fitting that this Shekinah Glory which disappeared over the Mount of Olives should now return in the person of the triumphant Jesus, the one who embodies the very glory of God.

From this mountain, Jesus ascended to heaven. And as the disciples were gazing up to heaven as he disappeared behind clouds, two angels appeared who asked, "'Men of Galilee,' they said, 'why do you stand here looking into the sky? This same Jesus, who has been taken from you into heaven, will come back in the same way you have seen him go into heaven'" (Acts 1:11). What the angels

EVEN THOUGH JUST A FEW SAW HIM LEAVE, BILLIONS—INDEED ALL WHO DWELL ON THE EARTH— WILL SEE HIM RETURN.

didn't say—though they surely could have—is not merely that Jesus would return but that He would return to the very place where He ascended. But even though just a few saw Him leave, billions—indeed all who dwell on the earth—will see Him return.

When Jesus returns, He comes to inflict judgment on His enemies. After the armies of the earth have been subdued, He will establish His promised kingdom. Read the rest of Zechariah 14, and you will find that it is filled with glorious symbolism. It describes living water flowing from Jerusalem; it predicts that the name of God will be inscribed on the bells of the horses, symbolic of the fact that God will be honored everywhere. This is descriptive of the millennial kingdom that we will discuss in more detail in the next chapter.

Then another dramatic event that will take place—a Jewish remnant will believe on Jesus. This passage in Zechariah must be quoted a second time: "And I will pour out on the house of David and the inhabitants of Jerusalem a spirit of grace and supplication. They will look on me, the one they have pierced, and they will mourn for him as one mourns for an only child, and grieve bitterly for him as one grieves for a firstborn son" (Zechariah 12:10). These Jews will deeply regret that they misread the evidence; they will repent of their unbelief and finally accept that Jesus was and is their Messiah.

Zechariah continues, "On that day a fountain will be opened

to the house of David and the inhabitants of Jerusalem, to cleanse them from sin and impurity" (13:1). Two-thirds of the people will be killed during the great tribulation, but as for the other third, "This third I will bring into the fire; I will refine them like silver and test them like gold. They will call on my name and I will answer them; I will say, 'They are my people,' and they will say, 'The Lord is our God'" (v. 9).

So it is that this remnant of Jews will be cleansed from their sins, and will enter into the millennial kingdom. Of course the kingdom will not only include Jews but Gentiles. All who trusted Christ as Savior and actually survived the tribulation will enter into this promised kingdom.

Now let us hear Jesus' description of the same event.

WHEN EVERY EYE SHALL SEE HIM

The glorious return of Jesus is both local (to the Mount of Olives) but also global. Let's listen to Jesus speaking in Matthew 24:27–28 about His own return: "For as lightning that comes from the east is visible even in the west, so will be the coming of the Son of Man. Wherever there is a carcass, there the vultures will gather."

We continue with a famous passage quoted in an earlier chapter:

Immediately after the distress of those days

"the sun will be darkened,
and the moon will not give its light;
the stars will fall from the sky,
and the heavenly bodies will be shaken."

At that time the sign of the Son of Man will appear in the sky, and all the nations of the earth will mourn. They will see the Son of

Man coming on the clouds of the sky, with power and great glory. And he will send his angels with a loud trumpet call, and they will gather his elect from the four winds, from one end of the heavens to the other. (vv. 29–31)

Yes, the coming of Jesus will be a spectacular worldwide event. John's revelation described it this way, "Look, he is coming with the clouds, and every eye will see him, even those who pierced him; and all the peoples of the earth will mourn because of him. So shall it be! Amen" (Revelation 1:7).

Of course we can ask how "every eye will see him" since the world is round and obviously it is not possible for the whole world to be able to see Jerusalem. Perhaps—and of course we do not know—television cameras would photograph the event and send the news around the world. Perhaps it is more likely that the return of Jesus is an event that takes place over a period of twenty-four or forty-eight hours. The sign of the Son of Man will appear in the sky and be seen by all as the world turns on its axis; then as the rotation continues, Jesus is continually seen as coming closer to the earth until eventually He disappears for the rest of the world as He lands on the Mount of Olives.

His return will be accompanied by convulsions in nature. The sun will be darkened, and since the moon only reflects the light of the sun, we should not be surprised to read that "the moon will not give its light." The stars of the heaven will fall. What a cataclysmic event!

We've noted that "the peoples of the earth will mourn because of him" (Revelation 1:7). As already mentioned, some will mourn because they recognize Jesus as Messiah; the Gentiles will also wail or mourn because of their sins. But all the people of the earth will know that Jesus has arrived bodily on Planet Earth, and that He has descended to the Mount of Olives.

GIVEN THE FRIGHTFUL EVENTS OF THE TRIBULATION, WE SHOULD NOT BE SURPRISED IF SOME CHRISTIANS WILL BE IN HIDING IN DIFFERENT PARTS OF THE WORLD.

Jesus also will employ angels to do His work for Him as He establishes His kingdom: "And he will send his angels with a loud trumpet call, and they will gather his elect from the four winds, from one end of the heavens to the other" (Matthew 24:31). Given the frightful events of the tribulation, we should not be surprised if some Christians will be in hiding in different parts of the world. The angels will find them and bring them to Jesus. Such an event seems strange to us, but remember when Lazarus died, "angels carried him to Abraham's side" (Luke 16:22). There is of course this difference: in the case of Lazarus, angels accompanied his soul to its destination; in this prediction, angels will gather the elect who will be in their earthly bodies and summon them to Jerusalem where the kingdom will be established.

No one who is alive on Planet Earth will miss the glorious return of Jesus. Whether they are punished for their rebellion or blessed with their salvation, either way the return of the King will not go unnoticed. He will return as promised.

And now we discover that we help form Christ's entourage in His glorious descent.

HIS GLORY, OUR GLORY TOO

Incredibly, we as believers will participate in our Lord's glorious appearing. Keep in mind that we will have already been raptured; we will have appeared at the judgment seat of Christ and will have been present for the marriage supper of the Lamb.

Of all the passages in the Bible, Revelation 19 is where we have the most detailed description of this monumental event—the glorious return of Jesus. We can scarcely fathom it. Revelation 19:11–16 describes:

I saw heaven standing open and there before me was a white horse, whose rider is called Faithful and True. With justice he judges and makes war. His eyes are like blazing fire, and on his head are many crowns. He has a name written on him that no one knows but he himself. He is dressed in a robe dipped in blood, and his name is the Word of God. The armies of heaven were following him, riding on white horses and dressed in fine linen, white and clean. Out of his mouth comes a sharp sword with which to strike down the nations. "He will rule them with an iron scepter." He treads the winepress of the fury of the wrath of God Almighty. On his robe and on his thigh he has this name written: KING OF KINGS AND LORD OF LORDS.

There's no doubt as to who is riding on the white horse; it is "The King of Kings and Lord of Lords"! Are we to believe that Jesus will be actually riding on a horse? Perhaps not. John received this revelation in the context of his own culture and familiar descriptions. Kings rode on white horses in ancient times, so it is only appropriate that King Jesus would be pictured as doing the same. Whether literal or not, the imagery is that of a victor, coming on a white horse, exercising unquestioned authority.

The name of Jesus is "Faithful and True." Although there are many different names that could have been selected for Jesus in this context, His faithfulness and trustworthiness are highlighted— because He is now keeping His promise of returning to earth. He is as good as His word.

> WILL HE BE THERE TO WELCOME US WHEN WE DIE? YES, FOR HE HAS PROMISED ETERNAL LIFE FOR ALL WHO BELIEVE.

Donald Grey Barnhouse, a pastor of another generation, said that there was an unconverted minister who was visiting a woman in the hospital who was about to die. She was so sure of heaven that the young minister felt that it was his responsibility to warn her about being presumptuous about her future after death. But she answered, "If, when I die, I find myself among the lost, God will have lost more than I will." The minister asked, "How so?" She replied, "I would have lost my soul, but He would have lost His good name."

Is Jesus believable? Are His promises true? Can you count on those promises even when He has delayed His coming for centuries? Is He faithful and true even when judgment is on its way? Will He be there to welcome us when we die? Yes, for He has promised eternal life for all who believe. When we believe His promises, we discover He is as good as His name.

NOW AT LAST IN HIS PRESENCE A BRIGHT LIGHT WILL SHINE INTO THE DARKNESS OF EVERY HUMAN HEART.

John continues his description: "His eyes are like blazing fire" (v. 12). These are the eyes that had to adjust to the dim light of a stable in Bethlehem. These are the eyes that wept over the city of Jerusalem. These are the eyes that looked with compassion at the sick, the weary, and the grieving. But now those eyes are like a flame of fire piercing every human heart.

Those eyes are symbolic of the omniscience, the all-knowing wisdom of Jesus. Every secret deed will be exposed. People will discover that nothing has ever escaped His sight. "All things are naked and opened unto the eyes of him with whom we have to do" (Hebrews 4:13 KJV). Now at last in His presence a bright light will shine into the darkness of every human heart. Nothing will escape His gaze.

Next, we read that "on his head were many crowns" (Revelation 12). In ancient times, when a king conquered a country he would then take the crown of the defeated king and would himself wear it as a symbol of his victory. Jesus has many crowns, for He has conquered every kingdom on the earth. The crowns of the kings of the world appropriately grace His head.

"He has a name written on him that no one knows but he himself" (v. 12). In ancient times, to name someone meant that you had authority over that person; and furthermore, a name signified a person's character. The fact that no one knows the name written on Jesus except He Himself means that no one else has the right to name Him and thus usurp authority over Him. He is, after all, the sovereign Lord of the new creation.

We are also told He will come wearing "a robe dipped in blood." That blood-stained robe is not a symbol of His death, but rather a symbol of coming judgment as the book of Isaiah makes very clear: "Why are your garments red, like those of one treading the winepress? 'I have trodden the winepress alone; from the nations no one was with me. I trampled them in my anger and trod them down in my wrath; their blood spattered my garments, and I stained all my clothing'" (63:2–3). Garments dipped in blood are a sign that severe judgment has arrived.

Let's not miss this: "The armies of heaven were following him, riding on white horses and dressed in fine linen, white and clean" (Revelation 19:14). Who are these armies of heaven arrayed in fine linen? Fortunately, we don't have to guess. In context, the marriage supper of the Lamb has been completed and believers were described as arrayed in "fine linen, bright and clean" (v. 8). And now we have a similar description of those who accompany Jesus back to earth. Obviously, this is a reference to believers whose sin has been covered, whose names were found in the Book of Life, and who have just had marvelous fellowship with their Lord and Savior.

Amazingly, we receive the same means of transportation as Jesus Himself. We, too, come on white horses, however symbolic that expression might be. Yes, we will return *with* Jesus. We follow Him as He descends to the Mount of Olives and begins to slay His enemies. We watch our Savior triumph and we participate in His spectacular victory.

There is no evidence that we will do any fighting; at least we are not told that we will have any weapons; and what is more, Jesus is more than capable of doing it all by Himself. He does not have to kill the wicked one by one; the sword that comes out of His mouth is the Word of God. "Out of his mouth comes a sharp sword with which to strike down the nations. 'He will rule them with an iron scepter.' He treads the winepress of the fury of the wrath of God Almighty" (v. 15). The one who spoke to the storm on Galilee and said, "Peace be still" and the winds obeyed Him; the one who spoke the word and Lazarus was raised from the dead—that same voice that spoke and the universe was created—that voice shall speak and His enemies will be slain. As Paul says, "The Lord Jesus will overthrow [Antichrist] with the breath of his mouth" (2 Thessalonians 2:8). One breath from the Holy Son of God and all His enemies find themselves helpless to fight back. No wonder we read that on His robe and on His thigh is written, "King of kings and Lord of lords." As Dr. Ronald Allen says, "In the Second Coming, the judgment will be done, not by water, not by flood, not by fire, nor by storm but by His own hand. Did you hear that?"[1] His judgment is swift and direct.

Jesus must never be put on the same shelf with Muhammad or Krishna or Buddha or any of the other spiritual leaders of other traditions. This Messiah is King of Kings and Lord of Lords, and stands above all the prophets of the world, over all the religions of the world, and over all the would-be Saviors of the world. At His birth, He came to redeem. Now He comes to judge and declare His supremacy.

The account concludes with a chilling description that might even offend our sensibilities, "And I saw an angel standing in the sun, who cried in a loud voice to all the birds flying in midair, 'Come, gather together for the great supper of God, so that you may eat the flesh of kings, generals, and mighty men, of horses and their riders, and the flesh of all people, free and slave, small and great'" (Revelation 19:17–18). Yes, this is a gruesome and horrifying description, but it reveals an important insight: the angel proclaims victory and invites the vultures to this supper even *before* Jesus has slain anyone by the word of His mouth. The angel knows that the victory of Jesus is assured. The battle hasn't begun, but even so it will soon be over. As someone has said, already *it's all over except the shooting*!

Appropriately, this chapter ends with the Beast and the false prophet being thrown into the lake of fire (v. 20). History as we know it is over, but a new chapter on Planet Earth will begin. The millennial kingdom is about to be established. At last, the promises given to David and verified by an angel to Mary will be fulfilled. A descendant of David will rule on his throne and administer justice and righteousness throughout the earth. We will turn our attention to this coming era in the next chapter.

REFLECTIONS FOR TODAY

Though the glorious appearing is future event, as we reflect on it, we are reminded of some powerful truths that should guide it in the days ahead. First, we must never forget that Jesus is a Lord who exercises both mercy and judgment. The sweet baby Jesus who was born in Bethlehem is the same Jesus who will one day destroy His enemies with the very breath of His mouth. There is more to the character of Jesus than just the "loving Jesus" most people know about. Seemingly, He appears to have endless compassion, but He's also a Jesus of judgment. In Him, perfect love and perfect justice coexist. It is not possible for us to overestimate Jesus Christ's hatred of sin. That's why there is such a tsunami of judgment

HIS LOVE FOR HIS CHILDREN IS LIKE THE LOVE THAT HE HAS FOR HIS FATHER, AND IN TURN HIS FATHER HAS FOR HIM.

executed at His glorious appearing. This is the Jesus no one will be able to ignore.

But on the other hand, the good news is that it's also not possible for us to exaggerate Jesus Christ's love for all those who believe on Him. In fact, His love for His children is like the love that He has for His Father, and in turn His Father has for Him. In fact, the one triune God loves us with the same love that exists between the members of the Trinity. As the Father loved Jesus from before the foundations of the world, so the Father has loved us (John 17:21).

Second, the glorious appearing highlights the beauty of our salvation. In Revelation 19 two suppers are described. On the one hand there is the marriage supper of the Lamb with indescribable beauty and fellowship for the redeemed, and on the other hand there will be vultures gathering for "the great supper of God." The contrast could not be more striking and more vivid. We are confronted with two different kinds of people with vastly differing destinations. Those clothed in white will attend the marriage supper of the Lamb; in contrast at the "great supper of God," those who will participate *are* the supper. Birds will feed on them.

Those clothed in the righteousness of Christ are received and welcomed by the Almighty, and those who do not have such a garment are rejected by God. Just think of the amount of sin covered by these white robes! And these robes, figuratively speaking, are given to us freely by faith in Christ.

Finally, to clarify, your eternal destiny is determined by what we do with the opportunities God gives us in this life. If we think we can approach God on our own record and come to Him in our own way, we will be lost; but blessed are those who know that our only hope is to be saved on the merits of Christ's grace. When I asked a man sitting next to me on a plane about where he expected to spend eternity, he replied, "Don't worry, I'm going to be okay before God . . . I will stand on my own record." Frightening.

In contrast with such misplaced faith we gladly sing "Hail, King Jesus!" and look forward to praising Him through all eternity. His glorious appearing inspires us to be faithful, for we know that tomorrow He wins. And we win too.

NOTES

1. Ronald Allen, "The Second Coming: What Are We Looking For?" in Charles R. Swindoll, John F. Walvoord, and J. Dwight Pentecost, eds., *The Road to Armageddon: A Biblical Understanding of Prophecy and End-Time Events* (Nashville: Word Publishing, 1999), 162.

CHAPTER EIGHT

THE KING REIGNS
IN HIS KINGDOM

The messianic Kingdom on earth is a vindication of God's creative activity. . . . The triumph of God over the satanic dominion of this planet is necessary for the glory of God. If there were no messianic age, if God simply picked up the redeemed remnant and took them to heaven, then we would have to conclude that God was unable to complete what he began.
—William S. LaSor

When we pray "Thy kingdom come," what are we praying for? What did Jesus have in mind when He asked us to pray for His coming kingdom, and how would we recognize this kingdom if it were to appear? And what would our role be in it?

The idea of utopia exists in every human heart. Every generation has looked forward to an idyllic time when men and women live in peace and prosperity. This has been the goal of every civilization, every political philosophy, and every sincere Christian.

Thomas More invented the word *utopia* in 1516 when he wrote a book by that title, but the vision of a time of harmony and freedom was in existence long before then.

The Bible describes a future utopia, but one very different from worldly descriptions that have come to us throughout history. The biblical vision includes the intervention of God, namely, the coming of Christ to earth to personally establish His kingdom. History has proven conclusively that man cannot bring in any form of utopia because sin permeates human nature. Selfishness, dishonesty, and distrust make the possibility of any such a golden age impossible. But when Jesus returns, the King of Kings will do what man cannot. And, incredibly, we as believers will be given a part to play in this new world order.

Thankfully, God will complete what He began. The devil will not have the last word on this planet. The very place where Satan was given authority to rule will eventually be ruled by Jesus Christ. God subjected the rule of this world to Adam who dropped the scepter, and God let Satan pick it up. And so, the second Adam—that is, Jesus—will reverse this sequence of events and claim the title to rule in triumph. "You made him a little lower than the angels; you crowned him with glory and honor and put everything under his feet" (Hebrews 2:7–8). In putting everything under Him, God left nothing that is not subject to Him. Yet at present we do not see everything "subject to him" (v. 8). Yes, eventually all things will again be subject to man, specifically the one man named Jesus. Where Satan won a victory, Jesus will triumph.

OLD TESTAMENT PREDICTIONS
OF THE COMING KINGDOM

The prediction of a coming kingdom on earth ruled by Christ was clearly revealed to David. God gave him this startling revelation saying that he would have a son who would build a temple, and who would be disciplined when he did evil. But there was much more to this prediction: "When your days are over and you rest with your fathers, I will raise up your offspring to succeed you, who will come from your own body, and I will establish his kingdom. He is the one who will build a house for my Name, and I will establish the throne of his kingdom forever" (2 Samuel 7: 12–13). Solomon fulfilled the first part of that verse, but most assuredly, the throne of his kingdom was not established forever. That word *house* means "genealogy" and the word *kingdom* means territory in Israel where David ruled.

Has this promise ever been fulfilled? I think not. David certainly did not rule "forever." God was speaking about a kingdom that would transcend David's and Solomon's era, and He predicted a coming king who would rule forever.

As further proof that this promise was not fulfilled in Old Testament times, we are again reminded that the angel Gabriel said to Mary, "You will be with child and give birth to a son, and you are to give him the name Jesus. He will be great and will be called the Son of the Most High. The Lord God will give him the throne of his father David, and he will reign over the house of Jacob forever; his kingdom will never end" (Luke 1:31–33). Has Jesus ever ruled over the house of David and over the tribe of Jacob? Certainly we must agree He has never ruled from Jerusalem and the territory over which David ruled. Clearly, this is a reference to the coming kingdom age.

In the Old Testament prophets there are many chapters devoted to the idea of a utopia where God's special king rules, and we have descriptions of a kingdom, the likes of which we have never seen. For example, Isaiah 2:2–4 says:

> In the last days
> the mountain of the Lord's temple will be established

as the chief among the mountains;
it will be raised above the hills,
  and all nations will stream to it.

Many peoples will come and say,

"Come, let us go up to the mountain of the Lord,
to the house of the God of Jacob.
He will teach us his ways,
  so that we may walk in his paths."
The law will go out from Zion,
  the word of the Lord from Jerusalem.
He will judge between the nations
  and will settle disputes for many peoples.
They will beat their swords into plowshares
  and their spears into pruning hooks.
Nation will not take up sword against nation,
  nor will they train for war anymore.

If you visit the United Nations building in New York and then walk cross the street to the plaza, you will see a wall with an inscription of only the last half of verse 4, which reads, "And they shall beat their swords into plowshares, their spears into pruning hooks; nation shall not lift up sword against nation, neither shall they learn war anymore." Why wasn't the first part of the verse included in this inscription? Obviously, it is because the first part of the verse predicts that Messiah shall usher in this rule (judge) and bring peace to the nations. The point to be made is that *the United Nations thinks it can accomplish the heady goal of peace without Christ's intervention and help.*

Tellingly, on the wall there is no chapter and verse given for this quotation, but under it is simply the name *Isaiah*. The wall itself is called the "Isaiah Wall," but there is no hint that his prophecy necessitates the coming of Messiah in order for it to be fulfilled. Quite possibly the architects did not give the reference in Isaiah, lest someone look it up in the Bible and discover that it was a Messianic passage! The United Nations may be doing many good things, but trust me, their agenda does *not* include establishing peace on earth under the authority of Jesus!

Let's consider another similar prediction of Isaiah:

And he will delight in the fear of the Lord.

He will not judge by what he sees with his eyes,
  or decide by what he hears with his ears;
but with righteousness he will judge the needy,
  with justice he will give decisions for the poor of the earth.
He will strike the earth with the rod of his mouth;
  with the breath of his lips he will slay the wicked.
Righteousness will be his belt
  and faithfulness the sash around his waist.

The wolf will live with the lamb,
  the leopard will lie down with the goat,
the calf and the lion and the yearling together;
  and a little child will lead them. (11:3–6)

The phrases, "the wolf will live with the lamb" and the "leopard will lie down with the goat" remind us that we are not yet in the era of the millennial kingdom. Today if a wolf were to lie down with the lamb, when the wolf got up we would discover that the lamb is missing! Isaiah is speaking about the rule of Jesus on earth in the coming kingdom. Peace will come—but only Christ can bring it to earth.

WHO'S IN AND WHO'S OUT?

Who will qualify to enter into this kingdom? All those who pass the test at "The judgment of the nations" discussed by Jesus in

IF THE RAPTURE AND THE GLORIOUS APPEARING HAPPENED SIMULTANEOUSLY, THERE WOULD BE NO NEED TO HAVE A JUDGMENT OF THE "SHEEP AND THE GOATS."

Matthew 25. To quote the words of Jesus, "When the Son of Man comes in his glory, and all the angels with him, he will sit on his throne in heavenly glory. All the nations will be gathered before him, and he will separate the people one from another as a shepherd separates the sheep from the goats. He will put the sheep on his right and the goats on his left" (vv. 31–33).

We should note in passing that this text is further proof of the pretribulation rapture of the church. If the rapture and the glorious appearing happened simultaneously, there would be no need to have a judgment of the "sheep and the goats." That separation would have already occurred when all believers were caught up into the clouds to meet King Jesus. The only plausible explanation is that there is a period of time between the rapture and the glorious return when people do come to trust in Messiah Jesus. Thus this judgment does not take place at the rapture, but rather it takes place after the tribulation just before the millennium.

The imagery of sheep and goats would have been familiar to the first-century listeners. Sheep and goats, I'm told, don't get along well. Sheep are usually quite docile whereas goats are very unruly, so in this context, the sheep enter the kingdom and the goats are cast out. Jesus explains the terms of the judgment:

> Then the King will say to those on his right, "Come, you who are blessed by my Father; take your inheritance, the kingdom prepared for you since the creation of the world. For I was hungry and you gave me something to eat, I was thirsty and you gave me something to drink, I was a stranger and you invited me in, I needed clothes and you clothed me, I was sick and you looked after me, I was in prison and you came to visit me." (Matthew 25:34-36)

Has Jesus changed the terms of salvation? Is He now teaching that we are saved by our deeds of kindness to the poor and those who are imprisoned? After all, He commends those who fed the hungry and visited the oppressed in prison and invites these to enter the kingdom, whereas those who neglected these good works go into everlasting destruction. "Then he will say to those on his left, 'Depart from me, you who are cursed, into the eternal fire prepared for the devil and his angels'" (v. 41).

There is a better explanation for these verses than to say that deeds of kindness save us. Remember that during the tribulation period the faithful do not take the mark of the beast, whether Jew or Gentile. These people will endure persecution; they will be jailed, and many killed. The Jews especially will be targeted for persecution and martyrdom. The righteous Gentiles will want to support their fellow brethren, the Jews, and will do whatever is needed to stand in solidarity with the Jewish people. These Gentiles will have proved their loyalty to Christ by the way they treated His "brothers" (v. 40). Their sacrificial kindness is not the *root* of their faith, but the *fruit* of their faith.

The bottom line is that only believers will enter into the kingdom that is about to be established. Both Jews and Gentiles who refused the mark of the beast will be found worthy to enter the kingdom and hear words of welcome from Jesus. As for the others, "They will go away to eternal punishment, but the righteous to eternal life" (v. 46).

WHAT WILL WE FIND IN THE KINGDOM?

What are some of the characteristics of this kingdom? One of them is most assuredly that Jesus rules. "I have installed my King on Zion, my holy hill" (Psalm 2:6). During this kingdom age the curse will be partially lifted, but not totally. "Never again will there be in it an infant who lives but a few days, or an old man who does not live out his years; he who dies at a hundred will be thought a mere youth; he who fails to reach a hundred will be considered accursed" (Isaiah 65:20). The point is that if you die at the age of a hundred in the kingdom, you're dying young; whereas today to die at the age of a hundred is to die very old. In the kingdom there will be health and longevity, but death itself will not be avoided. These predictions do not depict heaven as some interpreters allege. In heaven all people will have eternal, indestructible bodies that will not die; whereas in the kingdom, people live in natural bodies and die.

At Christmas one of our favorite carols is "Joy to the World." Most of us only know the first stanza, "Joy to the world, the Lord is come! Let earth receive her King." But when you read through stanzas two through four, you find a beautiful description of the millennial reign of Jesus. The third stanza reads, "No more let sins and sorrows grow, nor thorns infest the ground." Verse four includes, "He rules the world with truth and grace, and makes the nations prove the glories of His righteousness, and wonder of His love."

Today Jesus is not making the nations "prove" anything. Look carefully at a crop growing in a field and you will see plenty of weeds; perhaps even thorns will be infesting the ground. Read the newspapers and you will soon discover that no one is ruling the world with "truth and grace." So when we sing this carol, we should realize that the author, Isaac Watts, was not only thinking about the first coming of Jesus in Bethlehem but also His second coming when He will redeem the earth.

SATAN IS THROWN INTO THE ABYSS
Read this critical passage that sheds additional light on the nature and length of the kingdom reign. Note especially the binding of Satan and the time frame:

And I saw an angel coming down out of heaven, having the key to the Abyss and holding in his hand a great chain. He seized the dragon, that ancient serpent, who is the devil, or Satan, and bound him for a thousand years. He threw him into the Abyss, and locked and sealed it over him, to keep him from deceiving the nations anymore until the thousand years were ended. After that, he must be set free for a short time. (Revelation 20:1–3)

Satan is thrown into the Abyss, a holding place for evil spirits which for now will include Satan. Recall that demons asked Jesus to not cast them into the abyss. The lake of fire still awaits these evil creatures; for now they are being held for judgment. In being confined here, Satan is not yet being punished, but he is simply prevented from deceiving the nations. As the millennial kingdom is about to begin, Jesus in effect says to an angel, "I have a job for you to do. I'm going to empower you so that you can bind Satan with a chain and throw him into the pit." The chain is probably symbolic, but the point is that this angel has the key (authority) to open the Abyss and throw the devil into this bottomless pit. All that the angel has to do is say, "Satan, I am under God's authority. Come over here. We have a place for you. You're going to be incarcerated for a thousand years. Get into the pit right now!" We salute the absolute authority of Jesus and His angels over Satan! An unnamed angel, acting under divine authority can bind the evil one and put him away for a thousand years! So much for his vaunted pride and power.

WE SALUTE THE ABSOLUTE AUTHORITY OF JESUS AND HIS ANGELS OVER SATAN!

Six times in this chapter we read the phrase "a thousand years." Have you ever wondered where the idea arose that the kingdom is going to last a thousand years? It is based on this chapter which repeatedly mentions this length of time—hence the term *millennium* (meaning a thousand years). And if you believe as I do that Jesus will return in glory before the millennium, you are a *pre*millennialist.

There is another popular view called amillennialism, which teaches there will be no millennial reign as such. These Bible teachers tend to spiritualize the Old Testament promises regarding the kingdom and believe that the church (not Israel) will inherit these promises. They assume that the "throne of David" is actually Jesus ruling in heaven rather than on earth. Certainly David would have never understood God's promise in that way. And when the angel said to Mary that her son would inherit the throne of his father David, and "reign over the house of Jacob forever" she certainly could never have imagined that this was to be fulfilled in heaven and not on earth.

BELIEVERS RULE WITH CHRIST

During this millennium, Satan is bound and believers rule with Christ: "I saw thrones on which were seated those who had been given authority to judge" (v. 4). Who will rule with Jesus in the millennial kingdom? I believe there will be four different categories of people.

First, there will be the Old Testament saints. Daniel predicted that His holy ones were going to be ruling with him (7:27). This will include Abraham, Moses, David, and a whole host of other unnamed people saved in ancient times who will join in the rule with Christ during the millennial kingdom. I expect that Enoch who walked with God before the flood will also be raised to enter the kingdom.

Second, the apostles certainly will be ruling with Jesus. He gave them this special promise: "Jesus said to them, 'I tell you the truth, at the renewal of all things, when the Son of Man sits on his glorious throne, you who have followed me will also sit on twelve thrones, judging the twelve tribes of Israel' " (Matthew 19:28). We know that the eleven apostles will certainly rule with Christ.

And, lest you think we will be left out, the good news is that all present believers will also rule with Jesus. Paul writes, "If we endure, we will also reign with him" (2 Timothy 2:12). Jesus said to the churches of the book of Revelation, "He who overcomes, to him I shall grant to sit with me on my throne, even as I overcame and sat with my father on his throne." It also says in Revelation 5:10 that "You have made them to be a kingdom and priests to serve our God, and they will reign on the earth." We will be sitting with Jesus and carrying out the responsibilities that He gives us.

Finally, there is a fourth category: those believers who accepted Christ during the tribulation period and then either died a natural death or were martyred for their faith—these will be resurrected to reign with Christ. "I saw the souls of those who had been beheaded because of their testimony for Jesus and because of the word of God. . . . They came to life and reigned with Christ a thousand years. . . . This is the first resurrection" (Revelation 20:4–5). So, these saints join the others who will reign with Christ in the kingdom.

A point of clarification: When you read the above passage, just note that the word *this* in the phrase, "*this* is the first resurrection" actually refers back to the martyrs in verse 4 and does not include the dead who will be raised after the millennium to face judgment. In other words, the phrase, "The rest of the dead did not come to life until the thousand years were ended" (v. 5) is actually a parenthesis.

So, in John's mind, there are basically two resurrections. All those who participate in the "first resurrection" are believers: these include Jesus who was the first to be raised, then also the saints who were raised at the rapture, and now we can add to these those who died as martyrs in the tribulation period. And at some later period, there no doubt will be a resurrection of those who die in the millennium as believers. Obviously, the "first resurrection" is not just a one-time event but includes several resurrections. No wonder he writes "blessed and holy are those who have participated in the first resurrection."

The "second resurrection" is the resurrection of the unrighteous, those who will appear at the great white throne judgment. "The rest of the dead did not come to life until the thousand years were ended" (v. 5). These belong to the second resurrection, that is, the resurrection of those who will experience the "second death." The bottom line is that at one time or another all who die will be raised, either to everlasting life or everlasting damnation. All human beings will be eternal beings; all will have indestructible bodies, either enjoying eternal bless or suffering eternal damnation.

Are you troubled when you realize that in the millennial kingdom, those who have their eternal/resurrected bodies will be ruling over people who still have their earthly bodies? This interaction between the two kinds of people should not trouble us. After His resurrection, Jesus was able to interact with His disciples, and although in a glorified body, He ate fish with them (Luke 24:40–43; John 21:11–13). So, while it is difficult for us to imagine what life will be like in an entirely different sphere, we can trust the promises of God. We will rule with Christ in the kingdom and apparently intermingle with those who still struggle with the challenges of an earthly existence.

THERE IS A FINAL REBELLION

Incredibly, at the end of the millennium, Satan is released and foments a rebellion against God. "When the thousand years are over, Satan will be released from his prison and will go out to deceive the nations in the four corners of the earth—Gog and Magog—to gather them for battle" (Revelation 20:7–8). Don't confuse the terms Gog and Magog with the same names we discussed in chapter 6 where we expounded on some of the prophecies of Ezekiel. The timeline of this rebellion and the circumstances are totally different. Gog and Magog are sometimes used generally to refer to nations that are rebellious against God.

WE DON'T NEED THE DEVIL TO HELP US DO EVIL, THOUGH HE IS GLAD TO OBLIGE.

How could this rebellion happen in a peaceful environment under the leadership of Christ? Does this mean that believers can lose their eternal salvation and end in rebellion against Christ? A better explanation is that these people, the "sheep" who enter the millennial kingdom in their earthly bodies, will have children, and those children will grow up and some of them will trust King Jesus and others won't. Given their sin nature, they will be given the opportunity to express their opposition to Christ. This brief rebellion will be the final proof that human nature, even with Satan bound, will express itself in self-will and sustained rebellion. We don't need the devil to help us do evil, though he is glad to oblige.

As a contingent of rebels in this final battle arrives near the city of Jerusalem, God ends their foolishness by sending fire from heaven to destroy His enemies. Satan is then thrown into the lake of fire where the Beast and the false prophet already are, and "they will be tormented day and night for ever and ever" (v. 10). Never again will there be a rebellion on Planet Earth. The millennial kingdom is coming to an end, and a new era is about to begin, as we will discuss in chapter 10.

THE KINGDOM BECOMES ETERNAL

What next? With the era of the millennium now over, Paul tells us what happens: "Then the end will come, when he hands over the kingdom to God the Father after he has destroyed all dominion, authority and power" (1 Corinthians 15:24). In eternity past, God the Father in effect said to God the Son, "I'm going to give You a people to redeem." These are referred to as the elect; Jesus referred to them as "those you have given me." (See His repeated use of this phrase in John 17.) Jesus then comes and redeems His people by dying for them; He wins a massive victory over Satan, proving His superiority over all rivals. And, having completed His mission, and with all enemies now under His feet, He now triumphantly submits the kingdom to God the Father. And what does the Father do? Apparently the Father, deeply gratified by the Son's obedience, returns the kingdom back to the Son, because we are told that Jesus will rule forever and ever, "The kingdom of the world has become the kingdom of our Lord and of his Christ, and he will reign for ever and ever" (Revelation 11:15).

Perhaps it is better to say that God the Father and God the Son will share the eternal throne in Trinitarian glory and splendor. And we will be invited to join them and participate in this unimaginable honor. And to think, at this point in our experience, eternity will hardly have begun.

STRENGTH FOR TOMORROW

It is easy for us to read about the millennial kingdom, but it is quite different for us to grasp its reality. And, how can these truths transform us today? All of the Bible is relevant for us, and this is no exception. We must prepare for our distant future with the same diligence with which we plan for retirement, only more so.

First, let us remember what we learned about rewards. If we are faithful, we will be generously rewarded with a more honorable position in the kingdom. In a parable (Luke 19:11–27), Jesus indicated that there were differences of levels of faithfulness and therefore different levels of reward. In summary, after giving each servant a mina (about three month's wages), the king returned for an accounting: "The first one came and said, 'Sir your mina has earned ten more.' 'Well done, my good servant!' the master replied. 'Because you have been trustworthy in a very small matter, take charge of ten cities'" (vv. 16–17).

> TO LIVE FOR ONE'S SELF AFTER JESUS HAS GIVEN HIS LIFE FOR US IS AN INSULT TO OUR SAVIOR THAT WILL NOT GO UNNOTICED.

Then as the parable continues, the man whose mina made five more was put in charge of five cities. But the unfaithful servant, who hid his mina and refused to invest it, had his taken away from him and it was given to the servant whose mina had made ten minas. "I will judge you by your own words, you wicked servant! . . . Take his mina away from him and give it to the one who has ten minas" (vv. 22, 24). The point is that if you are faithful in this life you will be rewarded with special honors in the next. To live for one's self after Jesus has given His life for us is an insult to our Savior that will not go unnoticed.

Don't take it for granted that in the kingdom and the eternity that follows you will have the same honors as everyone else. The way we live in this life affects our position in the kingdom and, for that matter, all of eternity. Let us repent of our lack of passion in serving Christ. A victor at an ancient Greek Olympic game is said to have been asked, "Spartan, what will you gain by this victory?" He replied, "Sir, I shall have the honor to fight on the front line for my king." That determination should be ours as we fight for the King of Kings.

There is a second lesson, and that is the incorrigible nature of evil. A thousand years of incarceration do not change Satan's nature. He will come out of the Abyss just as evil and with just as much intent to fight against God as he had before he enters. He was probably even more enraged, because an evil being (or, for that matter, an evil person) doesn't change simply because he/she has been defeated. Hell is perfectly just for Satan who both will not and cannot repent of his rebellion against God. And those individuals who harden their own hearts and follow him will receive the same fate.

We've also seen that the children of human beings, though living under the authority of Jesus, will also rebel. In effect they will say, "Who is Jesus to rule over us? Yes, we took that field trip to Jerusalem. We saw that He is reigning there, and we see His far-reaching authority, but why should He be the one to choose what mansion we get to live in? We don't want Him to reign over us. We'd rather be free in hell than servants in the millennium!"

Think about this: As indicated, some of the children who grow up in the millennial kingdom will be "gospel hardened," as the saying goes. Living under the rule of Jesus, they will have heard it all and seen it all. They will reject His offer of eternal life in favor of their own rebellious ways. We must beware that we are not like them. "Today, if you hear his voice, do not harden your hearts. . . . See to it, brothers, that none of you has a sinful, unbelieving heart that turns away from the living God" (Hebrews 3:7–8, 12).

Things are not always what they appear to be. Satan, freed from his abyss, anxious to fight against Jesus one more time, will receive a whiff of satisfaction when he is released and foments a last rebellion against God. He will try to recruit as many as he can to join him in this last revolt against Jesus. But he and his accomplices will be defeated by Jesus using simply "the breath of his mouth." One breath and it will all be over.

Let us never forget that time is short and eternity is long.

CHAPTER NINE

THE KING JUDGES
UNBELIEVERS

*There is the dreadful pit of the glowing flames of the
wrath of God; there is hell's wide gaping mouth open;
and you have nothing to stand upon, nor any thing to take hold of.
There is nothing between you and hell but the air; 'tis only the
power and mere pleasure of God that holds you up. . . . You hang
by a slender thread, with the flames of divine wrath flashing about
it, and ready every moment to singe it and burn it asunder.*
—Jonathan Edwards

Jonathan Edwards's famous sermon, "Sinners in the Hands of an Angry God" (quoted above), is often reviled in today's tolerant and enlightened world. However, it is not within our power to create a God of our choosing; we must deal with the God who actually exists. And this God, revealed in the Bible, is gracious, merciful, and loving, but He is also just and finds sin abhorrent. And, yes, Edwards was right: hell exists and it is terrifying.

INSTEAD OF HARDENING OUR HEARTS AND SAYING, "HOW COULD GOD DO THAT?" WE SHOULD OPEN OUR HEARTS TO RECEIVE WHAT GOD SAYS ON THE SUBJECT.

Edwards's friend, missionary to the Indians David Brainerd, made the statement that more people come to saving faith in Christ through hearing the love of God preached than hearing the judgment of God preached. That might be true, but we can't grasp the love of God until we understand the judgment of God. His love and His justice share equally in His divine and perfect attributes. This chapter focuses on God's justice and His righteous anger against sin, and yes, His anger against sinners too.

The Bible says that God does not take pleasure in the death of the wicked (Ezekiel 18:23, 32). But He does judge sin wherever He finds it because His holiness and impeccable justice demand it. And in the end, this act of divine retribution also contributes to His eternal glory.

On an airplane, I sat next to an older woman and we struck up a conversation about religion and at one point in the discussion she said with an air of confidence, "If there is anything I know for sure, it's that hell doesn't exist." I replied somewhat wryly, "You know, you've put me in a really difficult dilemma, because on the one hand I wish you were right. But on the other hand, Jesus mentioned hell at least eleven times—that's more than the number of times He mentioned heaven. So you've put me in a predicament, because either I have to go with you, or I have to go with Jesus on this one. Don't feel too hurt, *but I'm going with Jesus.*"

On these matters, like most others, personal opinions don't count. So, instead of hardening our hearts and saying, "How could God do that?" we should open our hearts to receive what God says on the subject. And, if you are reading this and have no assurance that if you died today your destination would be heaven, you should especially seek to understand what God has revealed.

Without faith in Christ and God's grace extended to us, the description we are about to read would be the experience of us all.

A DESCRIPTION OF THE FINAL JUDGMENT

Read this passage carefully, and then I will attempt to explain its meaning:

> Then I saw a great white throne and him who was seated on it. Earth and sky fled from his presence, and there was no place for them. And I saw the dead, great and small, standing before the throne, and books were opened. Another book was opened, which is the book of life. The dead were judged according to what they had done as recorded in the books. The sea gave up the dead that were in it, and death and Hades gave up the dead that were in them, and each person was judged according to what he had done. Then death and Hades were thrown into the lake of fire. The lake of fire is the second death. If anyone's name was not found written in the book of life, he was thrown into the lake of fire. (Revelation 20:11–15)

This is the mother of all judgments. This is a judgment that is frightening, and yes, even chilling. As we consider the text, let us not only hear the words but imagine the scene. Think of tens of millions of people—perhaps billions—having to individually give an account of themselves on that terrifying day, with nothing to shield them from God's omnipotence and wrath.

First, we ask, who is the one who is seated on the throne? "I saw a great white throne and him who was seated on it." The throne is great because it is majestic; this after all, is the throne of God. This is the throne that exists from all of eternity. It is described as a white throne—absolute holiness, absolute purity. No one standing before it will be able to tweak their record to make themselves look better. There will be no possibility of bribery or bartering for an out-of-court settlement; they will appropriately cringe in the presence of the sovereign all-knowing judge who will adjudicate with thoroughness. No hidden facts. No extenuating circumstances, just vivid truth and searing justice. All who appear here will intuitively know that this Judge administers justly.

Since the Trinity is involved in all of God's works, we should not be surprised that we have references to God the Father and God the Son as ruling together in a passage like Revelation 5:13. "To him who sits on the throne and to the Lamb be praise and honor and glory and power for ever and ever!" Thus both the Father and the Jesus are described as ruling together. However, in this description of the great white throne, we should especially be thinking of Jesus as sitting on this throne, for He Himself told us, "Moreover, the Father judges no one, but has entrusted all judgment to the Son" (John 5:22). Paul, speaking of the day of judgment, said, "For he has set a day when he will judge the world with justice by the man he has appointed. He has given proof of this to everyone by raising him from the dead" (Acts 17: 21). Yes, Jesus is on that throne. The meek and mild baby Jesus whom people love at Christmas—the little baby who is thought of for a week and then put out of the minds of many during the rest of the year—this is the One who is on the throne. The redeemer has become the judge.

EARTH WILL BE INVISIBLE, NO GALAXY WILL BE IN SIGHT, AND THEY WILL BE STANDING IN LINE KNOWING THE JUDGMENT THAT AWAITS THEM.

Where is this throne? You'll notice that the text says that everything "fled from his presence, and there was no place for them" (Revelation 20:11). Now we have to think back to what we learned about the millennial kingdom. At the end, Jesus delivers the millennial kingdom to the Father, and evidently that kingdom transitions into the eternal kingdom. And it's during this period of transition that we have the fulfillment of the words of Peter: "But the day of the Lord will come like a thief. The heavens will disappear with a roar; the elements will be destroyed by fire, and the earth and everything in it will be laid bare" (2 Peter 3:10).

Scholars differ as to whether God will annihilate the present universe entirely and create a new one out of nothing, or whether the earth will be purified by fire and then re-created. Either way, when hordes of people are standing before the great white throne they will see nothing except the throne and He who sits on it. Earth will be invisible, no galaxy will be in sight, and they will be standing in line knowing the judgment that awaits them. If a defendant today stands before a judge in fear, not knowing how strictly he will be sentenced, we can multiply that terror by a thousand. Intuitively, each will know what awaits them. In the presence of the holiness of God and the white majestic throne, they will not have to wonder for long what is in store for their immediate future.

Let's look more carefully at the defendants. "I saw the dead, great and small, standing before the throne" (Revelation 20:12). Where did they come from? We learn that the sea gave up the dead that were in it, and death and Hades gave up their dead. They are all at the throne because God summons them from across the world and they must appear. No exceptions.

In ancient times it was said that if you drowned in the sea, sharks would eat you; if you were cremated and your ashes were sprinkled on the sea, then not even the gods could retrieve you. Thus, to be cremated was an inviting option since according to the folklore, you would be spared from judgment. So, cremation was like an insurance policy because the gods could not put you back together and call you to account.

Yet this is contradicted here where we learn that God will remember those who died in the sea and call them forth. On June

1, 1962 the cremated body of the Nazi butcher Adolf Eichmann was taken by an Israeli Navy patrol boat and thrown into the Mediterranean Sea beyond the territorial waters of Israel. The world was rid of him, but Eichmann still has an appointment with God. The body of Osama bin Laden, the evil mastermind of 9/11 and other terrorist attacks, was also thrown into icy waters. We are all relieved that his evil on earth has ended, but he also will be raised to give an account for his multiple crimes. The oceans will give up their dead when God speaks, and they will appear at His judgment seat and be appropriately punished in everlasting fire.

John MacArthur writes that "God knows every speck of human dust and every strand of DNA and he calls it forth from deserts, caves, jungles, seas, tombs, ghettos and palaces." They will all be there. Their bodies will be resurrected. Judgment day will have finally come.

In fact, no matter where bodies were buried, whether in land or sea, the dead will be raised for judgment. They will come from earthquakes where bodies have been destroyed and turned into dust. God will call them forth from coffins that were beautifully lined with satin, as well as those whose bodies were thrown away in tornadoes, floods, and famines. All unbelievers, that is, those who have never come under the protection of God's forgiveness and grace, will be resurrected to give account.

What else happens? We read that Hades "gave up the dead that were in them." When the unconverted die today, their body is buried but their soul goes to Hades, a place of torment. There they await final judgment. So, just as we as believers will have our souls join our bodies when the rapture takes place, just so in the case of unbelievers, their souls in Hades will join their new eternal resurrected bodies as they are readied for final judgment.

Let me clarify that Hades is not purgatory. The doctrine of purgatory was based on a faulty understanding of the doctrine of justification. The medieval belief was that no one dies righteous enough to enter heaven, so most people had to go to purgatory to be "purged from their sins" and then, hopefully, they would eventually be readied

HADES IS A REAL PLACE WITH REAL PEOPLE WAITING TO BE JUDGED AND THEN CONSIGNED TO A REAL HELL.

for heaven. But thankfully, the Bible teaches that the moment we believe on Christ we are declared righteous and fit for heaven. Purgatory does not exist.

However, in contrast, all who enter Hades (all unbelievers) will eventually be thrown into the lake of fire. Hades is a real place with real people waiting to be judged and then consigned to a real hell. They are fully aware of who they are and the details of their existence. At this point their travel plans cannot be rerouted; their fate is sealed.

We read that the small and great stood before God. John undoubtedly wants us to understand that this refers to people of different rank. A king is standing alongside those who died of poverty and sickness. Standing next to Hitler are good people who spent their lives helping the Jews escape from the terror of the Holocaust. Famous celebrities stand with the unknowns of this world; the wealthy stand with the poor. The aged stand alongside the younger generation. (I don't expect that children will be there, for "their angels in heaven always see the face of my Father in heaven," according to Matthew 18:10.)

There will also be diversity in the kind of works accomplished by these defendants. Yes, abusers will be there standing next to people who cared for the poor and ministered to the brokenhearted. The reason many "good" people will be present at this judgment day is because their good deeds did not, and could not earn a place for them in the heavenly kingdom. As they shall soon discover, their good deeds cannot protect them from the wrath to come. Only those who trust in Jesus, who Himself bore the wrath of God for those who believe in Him—only they are shielded from God's judgment. "Whoever believes in the Son has eternal life, but whoever rejects the Son will not see life, for God's wrath remains on him" (John 3:36).

Third, different religions will be represented. Protestants and Catholics, Buddhists and Muslims, people from among all of the religions of the world will be standing in line to await their sentencing. Hindus will be there, only to discover that their hope in reincarnation will not save them. Rather than entering another existence as another being, they will discover that they are standing awaiting judgment, and will remain who they are for all of eternity.

What unites these diverse people and brings them together? They have this in common: they lack the kind of righteousness God demands for entrance into heaven. Human goodness cannot save them; only the gift of divine goodness could have qualified them for a heavenly entrance. As Paul assured the believers in his day, "Since we have now been justified by his blood, how much more shall we be saved from God's wrath through him!" (Romans 5:9).

THE TIME FOR JUDGMENT HAS COME

Next comes the moment for the evaluation of these hapless individuals. The records will be examined. We are told, the "books were opened." We know that there will be at least two books used in the judgment: one containing all of their works, and then there is also the Book of Life. So the books will be opened, and each person will be shocked to discover that God has been keeping a meticulous record of all of their works, words, and thoughts, whether good or bad.

Of course the judgment will be highly personal and individual. "Each one" will be judged according to his or her works. To be a just judgment it must be a singular judgment, person by person. We don't know how long it will take God to do this because He does not have the same time constraints as we do. What we do know is that regardless of being in a different realm that we can hardly imagine, each person will have his or her moment before God.

So, with an open book, their works will be examined. What they did and what they said will be a part of the evaluation. As Jesus taught, "For by your words you will be acquitted, and by your words you will be condemned" (Matthew 12:37). And again, "But I tell you that men will have to give account on the day of judgment for every careless word they have spoken" (v. 36). Can you imagine the plight of those who swore and repeatedly used vulgar language? There will not be a single word or deed overlooked. It will all be there recorded in the book.

Even more telling, the secrets of the heart will be judged (Romans 2:16). Motives will be examined to expose what they did or didn't do and why. The lies that were told, the cover-ups, the anger, the selfish, envious, and lustful thoughts: all these will be exposed. No one will debate what God will reveal because they will know intuitively it is meticulously accurate.

> BECAUSE GOD IS JUST, THE STANDARD OF JUDGMENT IS GOING TO BE BASED ON WHAT THEY DID WITH WHAT THEY KNEW.

What is the standard of judgment? People will be judged on the basis of what they did with what they knew, based on their conscience, based on the light of nature, and based on whether or not they ever heard the gospel. Listen to the words of Paul, "All who sin apart from the law will also perish apart from the law, and all who sin under the law will be judged by the law" (Romans 2:12). He goes on to explain that the Gentiles who do not have the revealed law (such as Israel had), these pagans will not be judged by the law but by the light of conscience (vv. 14–15). Israel, the nation that received the law at Sinai, will be judged by the standards of that law, whereas the pagans will be judged by the light of nature.

I assume that millions who stand before God in this judgment will never have heard of Jesus Christ and the salvation that is available through Him. They will not hear God say, "I'm sending you to hell because you didn't believe on Jesus." That would be manifestly unjust. How could God hold people accountable to respond to a message that they never heard? Because God is just, the standard of judgment is going to be based on what they did with what they knew.

Intuitively, their conscience told them that lying was wrong, and yet they lied. They knew immorality was wrong and yet they were immoral. In other words, in a hundred ways they (much like the rest of us) squelched their conscience. It will be shown that nature gave them adequate proof of God's existence and power, and their conscience gave them the light of the moral law. Yet, they suppressed the truth and did what they knew was wrong. On the other hand, as for those who did hear the message of Christ and rejected it, needless to say their condemnation will be greater.

Jesus made the statement that it will be more bearable for Sodom and Gomorrah in the day of judgment than it will be for those cities that rejected Him when He was here on earth (Matthew 10:15). Why? The greater the light, the greater the judgment. M. R. DeHaan, a Bible teacher of another era, said that for the headhunter who never heard of Jesus, his hell will appear as heaven in comparison with the person who listened to the gospel and hardened his heart against it and did not believe. Imagine being haunted for all eternity with memories of opportunities squandered.

Alas, however, the book that records human deeds is read only for the purpose of condemnation. The record will testify against all who appear at this judgment. However, as we have emphasized, there will be degrees of punishment. The severity of the evil will be balanced against the amount of knowledge a person had of right and wrong and of the gospel message. In the lineup before the throne, Hitler might be standing with some compassionate person who bravely opposed his evil deeds, but once the individual judgments are over, the two will be consigned to very different levels of punishment. To quote Jesus on this topic, "From everyone who has been given much, much will be demanded; and from the one who has been entrusted with much, much more will be asked" (Luke 12:48). Responsibility is based on knowledge. The one who knows God's ways will be punished more than the person who didn't. It will all be just.

Sin will be judged on its own merits, but also its impact in the lives of others will be taken into account. Jesus taught that if you cause a child to stumble, it would be better for you if you were drowned in the sea (Matthew 18:6). This doesn't just apply to child abusers. Think of the responsibility of parents, and how important it is that they direct their children in the right way. If the parent causes a child to stumble in his or her faith in Christ— if the parents turn the child away from God's path—they will pay the consequences.

Consider a man who is committed to immorality. He destroys the lives of all the women he meets through his lies, his betrayal, and his artificial persona. For that he will be judged. But suppose he is a narcissist who glamorizes sexual perversity and wants to multiply his sin by becoming a pornographer, so he publishes a magazine that is looked at (and supposedly read) by millions of young men whom he seeks to lead into a lifestyle akin to his own. They are now as committed to immorality and degrading women as the pornographer himself. As for the pornographer, he continues to appeal to a younger audience, hoping that he can entice more men to become addicted to his pornography. He is wildly successful and gloats over his glamorous lifestyle and lack of shame. He boasts about evil as if it is good. As Paul so accurately put it, there are those who not only do evil but take delight in others who join them in their evil ways. (Romans 1:32). Such a man will incur a much more severe judgment for encouraging millions to defile themselves with sinful sexual relationships.

False teachers will also incur a stricter judgment. It's one thing to be wrong about the finer disputed points of doctrine, but it is quite another to teach heresy and lead others astray regarding the nature of salvation. No wonder James says teachers will have a stricter judgment (James 3:1). The bottom line: All of God's punishment will be meticulously meted out in accordance with what they did or didn't do with what they knew to be right and good.

THE SENTENCES ARE ANNOUNCED

Next comes the sentencing itself. We must now turn our attention from the book of condemnation to the book of life. "If anyone's name was not found written in the book of life, he was thrown into the lake of fire" (Revelation 20:15). This is the book that lists the names of the redeemed. This book lists those who were purchased by Christ and belong to Him. And, as far as we know, none of the defendants who appear before the great white throne judgment has his or her name written in this book. As we have learned in chapter 2, the redeemed do not appear at this judgment but are judged at the "judgment seat of Christ" (2 Corinthians 5:10).

Let's imagine that someone at the great white throne judgment were to argue with God saying, "Look at Your list again! My name should be in the Book of Life . . . did I not do good works in Your name? Did I not cast out demons in Your name and in Your name do many wonderful works?" (see Matthew 7:21–23). And the Lord will say to them, "I never knew you. Away from me, you evildoers!" And so it will be that these deceived souls will be told that their names are not inscribed in the book of life. Thus we read, "If anyone's name was not found written in the book of life, he was thrown into the lake of fire" (Revelation 20:15).

IS GOD OVERREACTING TO THEIR SIN? IS THEIR PUNISHMENT GREATER THAN THE CRIME?

Is God overreacting to their sin? Is their punishment greater than the crime? Sure, they sinned against God; yes, they did some evil things, but don't we all? In reply to this question, consider this: What if, as the theologian Jonathan Edwards believed—what if the greatness of the sin was dependent on the greatness of the person against whom it was committed? When I was a boy growing up on the farm, we as children would throw snowballs at one another. That was not considered worthy of a reprimand, but let's suppose you were to throw a snowball at the mailman. You might be in a bit of trouble. If you threw it at a policeman, that would be even more serious. If you threw a snowball at the president of the United States, you would be arrested and jailed. The higher we go up the ladder of greatness and importance, the more culpability we have for our sin. Now think of the fact that all of our sins are against a holy, transcendent, pure, eternal, omnipresent, omnipotent God who created us. That makes even so-called small sins a serious infraction. Simply put, it is not possible to exaggerate how offensive our sin is toward God.

Why is the lake of fire eternal? All human beings will have eternal, indestructible bodies and will therefore live somewhere eternally. Either we will be rejoicing in the presence of God or we will be in the lake of fire. The real you—the person you are—will live forever.

Will the fire of hell be literal? We can't know for certain because although hell is described as the lake of fire, hell is also spoken of as "outer darkness." However, even if fire is symbolic it has to be symbolic of something—something horrendously awful—and eternal. Certainly the regrets people have will be eternal, as Dante said in his *Inferno*, "Abandon all hope, ye who enter here."

EXAMINE YOURSELF

The multitudes who find themselves at the great white throne judgment lacked the righteousness needed for entry into heaven. On the other hand, those who have trusted Christ as Savior, while alive on earth, "settled out of court." They took Jesus up on His promise, "For God so loved the world that he gave his one and only Son, that whoever believes in him shall not perish but have eternal life. For God did not send his Son into the world to condemn the world, but to save the world through him" (John 3:16–17). Today, it is not too late to take advantage of what Jesus, in effect, says to us: "If you believe that My death was a sacrifice for sinners; if you believe that I bore your hell when I died on the cross; if you trust your eternal soul to me, you will be exempt from eternal punishment and you will be welcomed into the kingdom of My Father."

Why does our faith have to be in Jesus? No one else is qualified to be a Savior. Buddha didn't claim to be a savior; Krishna didn't claim to be a Savior; Muhammad didn't claim to be a Savior. Because Jesus is both God and man, He's the only one able to die in our place and have His sacrifice accepted by God the Father, and then, praise be, He gives us the gift of divine righteousness. He gives us many gifts, but the two most important are forgiveness and righteousness. On that basis, God repeatedly affirms through His promises that if we trust His Son, we will be just as welcome in heaven as the Son Himself. No wonder Stephen, the first Christian martyr, saw heaven open to receive him before he died (Acts 7:55–56). Jesus was in effect saying, "Stephen, be faithful, because when you die I'm up here for you." Most assuredly, Stephen will not be at this day of judgment, and neither will you and neither will I if we transfer our trust to Christ even as he did.

A friend of mine said he saw a bumper sticker that read, "He died in 33 AD. Get over it!" Rather than such blasphemy, the bumper sticker should read, "He died in 33 AD. He was raised three days later. He's coming again. Don't ever get over it."

If I die in a hospital, I want it to be to the strains of one of my favorite songs: "Just as I Am, Without One Plea." As you read these words let them be your prayer.

Just as I am, without one plea
But that thy blood was shed for me,
And that thou bidd'st me to come to thee,
O Lamb of God, I come, I come.

Why this song? A famous preacher was dying, struggling with doubts about what awaited him. His friends tried to console him, but he refused to be comforted. Then, he was reminded that our basis for entry into heaven has nothing to do with our performance, but everything to do with what Christ did for us. When he was reminded of the blood of Christ, he died in peace.

Luther put it so aptly, "O, Lord, I am thy sin and thou art my righteousness."

That is the gospel. If we believe that, we cannot come into condemnation; without it we will be condemned forever. Our eternal destiny depends on our relationship with Jesus Christ.

O Lamb of God, I come!

CHAPTER TEN

THE KING INVITES US
TO REIGN WITH HIM

*The curtain of Revelation drops with the final vision of
glorification. The glorified shall reign forever and ever.
It is a reign! That is, it is a condition of complete glorification.
It is a condition of perfect sharing in the wonder of God.
And it is eternal. It will last forever and ever. And thus, the
vision ends with the redeemed in a state of eternal glory
reigning with God and the Lamb.*
—Bernard Ramm

Welcome to eternity.

Life, as it once existed on earth, is over. Jesus has come
back as promised to receive His church; He has also returned in
glory to the Mount of Olives to establish His long-awaited kingdom. He has ruled on earth for a thousand years, and Satan, the
Beast, and the false prophet have been thrown into the lake of
fire, along with their followers. And now that all His enemies

have been vanquished, He presents the kingdom to the Father, and together They have begun their rule in Trinitarian harmony and bliss. And in this eternal state, you and I have a part to play.

This chapter stands in stark contrast to the previous one. We've just spoken of a terrifying judgment, when the judge of all the ages will personally judge all unbelievers who will be thrown into "the lake of fire." If the suffering of those whose names were not found in the Book of Life is beyond our imagination, just so the glory that awaits all those who have the privilege of ruling with Christ is beyond our imagination.

THOSE WHO RECEIVE THE RIGHTEOUSNESS OF CHRIST BY FAITH IN HUMBLE REPENTANCE ARE WELCOMED INTO HEAVENLY BLISS AS IF THEY WERE CHRIST.

Why the two radically divergent destinations? I repeat again that this has nothing to do with some people being "better" than others as the term is most often used; it is not a matter of pride on the part of some, thinking they were wise enough to prepare for eternity. The difference has entirely to do with their relationship with Jesus Christ. We are all born in sin; we are all worthy of the lake of fire, we are all helpless sinners. But those who receive the righteousness of Christ by faith in humble repentance are welcomed into heavenly bliss as if they were Christ. No wonder Paul says, "we preach Christ and not ourselves."

There are three reasons for this chapter. First, to give us a glimpse into eternity and what our eternal home will be like. I think it was C. S. Lewis who said that our ability to imagine what eternity will be like is two infants in a womb talking about what they will be doing once they are born and are twenty-five years old. In other words, we must realize that eternity is an entirely different realm of existence; we can read the Scriptures and visualize the descriptions, but ultimately we can't "get our minds around it," as the saying goes. However, God has revealed enough to us to invite us to contemplate its beauty and above all, the intimacy we will share with our triune God. Yes, we will have a role in that new kingdom, though it is beyond our ability to grasp.

Second, I hope that those of you with heavy burdens, whether physical, financial, emotional, or otherwise, will be reminded of the glories of eternity that lie ahead. As Paul wrote, "I consider that our present sufferings are not worth comparing with the glory that will be revealed in us" (Romans 8:18). Life is hard, but eternity is coming.

Before her death at age 103, I called my mother every Saturday evening. During our conversation a few weeks before her death, she asked me a question she'd often ask, "What are you going to preach about tomorrow?" I said, "Mother, I am going to speak about heaven," and immediately she said, "Oh, that will be glorious," and then she began to quote a poem in German about the beauty and glory of heaven. She was anxiously awaiting the time when she could lay her burdens down and enter into glory. Of course when she died, she did not as yet enter into the final heaven, which awaits the consummation of the end of the age. As of now, the New Jerusalem has not yet descended to earth (Revelation 21:1–5). But I write this chapter to encourage us to be faithful, no matter how old or burdened we might be.

I WRITE THIS CHAPTER TO ENCOURAGE US TO BE FAITHFUL, NO MATTER HOW OLD OR BURDENED WE MIGHT BE.

A third reason for this chapter is to provide one last warning for those who, if they died today, would not spend their eternity in the Holy City. In fact, in the description of the New Jerusalem there is one last warning that some people will find themselves outside the gates, unable to gain entry. The decision as to who is in and who is out is made by God. But we are not left wondering why some are within the city and why some are judged unworthy of entrance. Let me say it again: it has to do with our relationship with Jesus Christ.

A FIRST GLIMPSE OF THE NEW JERUSALEM

But before this warning there is an astonishing description based on John's remarkable vision of events that will yet unfold in the coming future. Revelation 21:1–4 should be read with great care:

> Then I saw a new heaven and a new earth, for the first heaven and the first earth had passed away, and there was no longer any sea. I saw the Holy City, the new Jerusalem, coming down out of heaven from God, prepared as a bride beautifully dressed for her husband. And I heard a loud voice from the throne saying, "Now the dwelling of God is with men, and he will live with them. They will be his people, and God himself will be with them and be their God. He will wipe every tear from their eyes. There will be no more death or mourning or crying or pain, for the old order of things has passed away."

Let's give thoughtful consideration to this incredible description. We read, "I saw a new heaven and a new earth." Remember that during the period between the millennial kingdom and eternity, the earth will be destroyed as Peter tells us (2 Peter 3:10–13). As already indicated, theologians debate as to whether the Bible teaches the world as we know it will be obliterated and re-created, or simply remade, purified by fire. Either way, this will be a *new* heaven and a *new* earth, a brand-new universe that will be free from every single taint of sin and curse. This New Jerusalem that will come down as a bride adorned for her husband is the eternal state of the redeemed. This will be heaven—*forever*.

Believers today are with Christ, but they need to be raised with their glorified bodies. The events I've attempted to detail in this book will have to have happened before the New Jerusalem descends to earth. This city, which will be adorned as "a bride for her husband," will be exquisite in its beauty and glory. This bride outshines them all.

J. Vernon McGee, an old Southern preacher who is now with the Lord and awaiting entrance into the New Jerusalem, used to joke, "I believe that God does a miracle because every bride is **GOD WILL GET TO THE VERY HEART OF WHAT TROUBLED US ON EARTH.** beautiful on her wedding day!" Well, miracle or not, *this* bride certainly will be full of beauty, adorned for her husband. The New Jerusalem will be sparkling, and scintillating. "No eye has seen, no ear has heard, no mind has conceived what God has prepared for those who love him" (1 Corinthians 2:9). Yes, Paul does go on to say that God has revealed our future to us by His Spirit, but we grasp only a glimpse of it here.

WHAT WILL BE MISSING IN THE NEW JERUSALEM

What will be missing in the New Jerusalem? Absent will be (1) tears, for God Himself shall wipe them from our eyes (v. 4). Interestingly, the Greek text says literally that God will wipe our tears "out of our eyes" as if to imply that every single bit of sorrow and every bit of regret will be wiped away. The point is that God will get to the very heart of what troubled us on earth. It's not as if God will necessarily take a tissue and wipe our tears away. Rather, He will give us understanding about His ways and purposes. He will remind us that our sin is paid for—and as for those who are not in heaven whom we hoped would be there, He will take away the cause of our sorrow by helping us see that He did all things justly. We will be content with what God has done, and all sorrows will be removed forever.

Then (2) "there will be no more death or mourning or crying or pain, for the old order of things has passed away" (v. 4).

FINALLY THERE WILL BE RELIEF FOR ALL SUFFERING "FOR THE OLD ORDER OF THINGS HAS PASSED AWAY."

As a pastor I know that I will no longer need to preach the gospel in heaven; and if you are a funeral director you most assuredly will have a new vocation. But if you are a choir director, you just might be able to continue leading praises of worship and adoration. No death, no sorrow, no sickness, no parting, no goodbyes.

Do you live with chronic pain? Do you suffer from migraines that make you wish you could die? Or a debilitating disease that makes you scream, saying you can't take it anymore? My friend, your day of healing is coming. There will be "no mourning or crying or pain." Finally there will be relief for all suffering "for the old order of things has passed away." This should bring joy to the heart of every struggling believer.

THE RESIDENTS OF THE NEW JERUSALEM

Who dwells in the New Jerusalem? First, and most importantly, this is the dwelling place of God. "Now the dwelling of God is with men, and he will live with them" (v. 3). Some older translations say that "the tabernacle of God is with men." Whether we say "dwelling place" or "tabernacle," the idea is clear: just as God dwelt among His people in the tabernacle in the Old Testament era, just so He now dwells with His people in heaven. The difference is that sin is now no longer a barrier between us and God, thus we can dwell with Him in His holy abode and commune with Him without a mediator.

In Old Testament times the tabernacle was divided into an outer court where sacrifices were offered; the holy place where priests could freely move; and behind the veil, the Holy of Holies, where the priest was allowed to enter only one day of the year, the Day of Atonement. This arrangement was set up by God so that He could have fellowship with His people without Himself being contaminated. The question that dominates the story line of the Bible is: How can God have fellowship with sinners without Him compromising His holiness or destroying mankind because of his sin? So God said, in effect, "Even though I exist everywhere throughout the whole universe, I will be localized in the Holy of Holies. That is where My Glory will be seen." And, with the right sacrifices, the priests in the Old Testament were able to approach God on behalf of all the people. The congregation itself had to stay away from the exact place where God dwelt.

Now, this tabernacle—a heavenly one—is instantly accessible for all of us. And if we keep in mind that the Holy of Holies where the ark (mercy seat) was kept was a cube, we should notice that the New Jerusalem itself is also a cube (Revelation 21:16). So, when we are in the New Jerusalem, we are really dwelling in the Holy of Holies with God. We are in the inner sanctum, the inner shrine where God Himself dwells. For us today, God dwells in unapproachable light (1 Timothy 6:16), but in that day God will not only be approachable, He will be among us. With sin forever removed, we will be before His face continually. Our fellowship with one another and with Him will be uninterrupted and spontaneous.

THIS WILL BE OUR FIRST EXPERIENCE WITH UNCREATED LIGHT.

So now we understand why there will be no temple in the New Jerusalem, for it will be entirely unnecessary. "I did not see a temple in the city, because the Lord God Almighty and the Lamb are its temple. The city does not need the sun or the moon to shine on it, for the glory of God gives it light, and the Lamb is its lamp" (Revelation 21:22–23). This will be our first experience with uncreated light. This light will not emanate from the sun because, after all, God Himself is light, and since He is uncreated, the light that shines forth from Him is also uncreated. Our direct access to Him will have no barriers and no interruptions.

Joni Eareckson Tada, you will recall, has been a quadriplegic throughout her adult life. She has suffered greatly yet blessed millions because of what she has taught us about suffering. I remember her saying, "The thing that I look forward to when I get to heaven is not that I will be able to park my wheelchair in the vestibule of heaven and be able to run to Jesus to worship Him . . . what I will like the best, and what will be most meaningful, is instant continual communication with God *without a hint of sin ever coming between us.*" Yes, that is heaven.

Imagine your mind so pure that you wouldn't mind if your wife or your husband or even your children knew your every single thought. There will be no guilt and no shame, only purity, for the "pure in heart . . . will see God" (Matthew 5:8). God will dwell with His people in the New Jerusalem with uninterrupted joy and fellowship.

THE DESCRIPTION OF THE NEW JERUSALEM

Let's take a moment to look at this city's description. John is taken to a great and high mountain and shown the Holy City, the New Jerusalem that came down from heaven. We are told:

> And he carried me away in the Spirit to a mountain great and high, and showed me the Holy City, Jerusalem, coming down out of heaven from God. It shone with the glory of God, and its brilliance was like that of a very precious jewel, like a jasper, clear as crystal. It had a great, high wall with twelve gates, and with twelve angels at the gates. On the gates were written the names of the twelve tribes of Israel. There were three gates on the east, three on the north, three on the south and three on the west. The wall of the city had twelve foundations, and on them were the names of the twelve apostles of the Lamb. (Revelation 21:10–14)

Although we've all heard many jokes about Peter guarding

the "pearly gates" of heaven, unsurprisingly, he is not mentioned here as the custodian of heaven's door! The text says that twelve angels are at the twelve gates, and on the gates are the names of the twelve tribes of Israel. There we see a representative group of Old Testament saints. And then to complete the picture, we see twelve foundations with the names of the twelve apostles. Even in this city there will still be some distinction between Israel and the church, but at the same time all peoples are together in the New Jerusalem; all the saints of all ages enjoying God.

Verses 15–17 reveal details regarding the size of the city. We read:

> The angel who talked with me had a measuring rod of gold to measure the city, its gates and its walls. The city was laid out like a square, as long as it was wide. He measured the city with the rod and found it to be 12,000 stadia in length, and as wide and high as it is long. He measured its wall and it was 144 cubits thick, by man's measurement, which the angel was using.

Apparently, its length will be the same as its width. The angel measured the city with a rod and the total length was 12,000 stadia. Generally it can be said that this particular "stadium" unit of measurement might be more than a mile long. If that is correct, then the length would be approximately 1,500 miles; and since its height and length are equal, we can assume it would be a cube. Can you imagine a city extending from Colorado to the Atlantic Ocean and from the northern part of the United States all the way to the Mexican border, and towering 1,500 miles high? It would have room for billions of people, each with plenty of space![1]

When we think of the "streets of the city" we think of streets being horizontal. Yet we must keep in mind that in the New Jerusalem we will exist with glorified bodies. The Bible says that when we see Christ "we shall be like him, for we shall see him as he is" (1 John 3:2). We are assured that when Jesus comes, He will "transform our lowly body to be like his glorious body" (Philippians 3: 21 ESV). This means that we will be able to move vertically just as easily as we'll be able to travel horizontally. So perhaps the streets of the city are just as perpendicular as they are horizontal. Either way, whether up or down, it will not matter because we will be able to travel by just choosing to be in one place rather than another. Travel will be that effortless—and just imagine, you will need no sleep because your body will never need rest.

GOD IS A BUILDER WHOSE GLORY SHINES IN ALL HE CREATES.

Consider also the materials of the city:

> The wall was made of jasper, and the city of pure gold, as pure as glass. The foundations of the city walls were decorated with every kind of precious stone. The first foundation was jasper, the second sapphire, the third chalcedony, the fourth emerald, the fifth sardonyx, the sixth carnelian, the seventh chrysolite, the eighth beryl, the ninth topaz, the tenth chrysoprase, the eleventh jacinth, and the twelfth amethyst. The twelve gates were twelve pearls, each gate made of a single pearl. The great street of the city was of gold, like transparent glass. (Revelation 21:18–21)

Of course, we must keep in mind that much of this description might be symbolic. John had to put his vision into human words; he had to describe what he saw in the language that was available to him. However, it is obvious that God is a God of beauty. Even the plans He gave Moses to build the tabernacle indicate that He wanted a beautiful structure that was a credit to His own creative genius. Abraham looked forward to a city "whose architect and builder is God" (Hebrews 11:10). God is a builder whose glory shines in all He creates.

OUR PRIVILEGES IN THE NEW JERUSALEM

Although the privileges reserved for the occupants of this marvelous dwelling place are beyond our ability to grasp, we know that there will be equality in access. "The nations will walk by its light, and the kings of the earth will bring their splendor into it" (v. 24). In ancient times when a king had to submit to one who was greater and stronger than he, that defeated king would lay whatever he had at the feet of the victorious emperor. So it is only appropriate that the kings of this world, along with the "glory and honor of the nations," will be brought and laid at the feet of King Jesus. There will be no nationalism in this city, for even those who were great on earth will have to submit all they have to the King of Kings. At this point, whether we have much or little, it will not matter, for all belongs to Him whom we will now serve with gratitude and joy.

> WHETHER WE HAVE MUCH OR LITTLE, IT WILL NOT MATTER, FOR ALL BELONGS TO HIM WHOM WE WILL NOW SERVE WITH GRATITUDE AND JOY.

No need for diets, vitamins, or drugs. Excellent health for us all is on the way! "Then the angel showed me the river of the water of life, as clear as crystal, flowing from the throne of God and of the Lamb down the middle of the great street of the city. On each side of the river stood the tree of life, bearing twelve crops of fruit yielding its fruit every month. And the leaves of the tree are for the healing of the nations" (22:1–2). From the throne comes a river of water of life flowing right down the middle of Main Street; and, on the other side of the river stands the tree of life. That word *healing* in Greek means "health-giving."

Remember that the "tree of life" was first mentioned in Genesis 2, when God placed Adam and Eve in Eden and told them to not eat from "the tree of the knowledge of good and evil." When they disobeyed and were expelled from the garden, God would not let them return to paradise. God said, "He must not be allowed to reach out his hand and take also from the tree of life and eat, and live forever" (Genesis 3:22). If they had eaten of the tree of life as sinners, they would have been condemned to live forever in their sinful condition. Death actually was a divine gift that would allow them to escape from earthly existence and be fully restored to God's presence as a redeemed people.

Today, people go to great lengths to extend their life. You'd think that we want to live forever. But no matter how appealing a long life might be, we would not want to be locked into this earthly existence. Sin brings disease, pain, disappointment, broken relationships, and thankfully, eventually death. An eternal, miserable existence would not be a blessing but a curse.

But now in the New Jerusalem, with the curse forever lifted, we *can* "eat of the tree of life," a tree that is in perpetual bloom and "health-giving." We might wonder why we would want to eat in heaven, since we know our bodies will never become weary or sick. We will be blessed with limitless energy and boundless strength to do whatever God expects of us. Of course in heaven we will not eat because we *have* to, but because we *want* to; we will eat for sheer enjoyment. Earlier in the book of Revelation John writes, "Never again will they hunger; never again will they thirst. The sun will not beat upon them, nor any scorching heat. For the Lamb at the center of the throne will be their shepherd; he will lead them to springs of living water" (7:16–17). Eating and drinking will be a form of fellowship, a renewal of our dependence on and gratefulness to God.

Third, we will be active, doing God's will as instructed. "No longer will there be any curse. The throne of God and of the Lamb will be in the city, and his servants will serve him" (22:3). The word translated "serve" is the word generally used of the service within a temple or within a church gathering; it is the service of worship. In fact, everything we do in the New Jerusalem will be but a different form of grateful worship. We will also be reigning with Christ: "There will be no more night. They will not need the light of a lamp or the light of the sun, for the Lord God will give them light. And they will reign for ever and ever" (22:5). That expression "for ever and ever" is the strongest expression for eternity. Literally it says we will "reign into the ages of the ages." *Forever* is a long time.

A friend of mine once quipped, "I'm glad I'm not the events coordinator in heaven." His point was that many millions—if not billions—of activities would have to be planned if we are to be active forever. Surely, we think, God Himself will run out of things for us to do after say, the first billion years.

I read about a cartoon from *The Far Side* with a picture that typifies many people's view of heaven. A man adorned with angel's wings sits on a cloud playing a harp. His face looks as if he's just been marooned on an island and is bored out of his mind. The caption reads, "I wish I had brought a magazine!"

OUR INFINITE GOD WILL NOT RUN OUT OF IDEAS AND WILL HAVE PLENTY OF ASSIGNMENTS FOR US TO DO.

In heaven we will be glad that we have brought nothing with us. We will not gather for a long church service where we begin on page one of the hymnal and sing our way through, and then when finished begin the process over again. We will be busy serving the Lord, and His name will be on our foreheads. We are not sure all that will be entailed in our reign with Christ, but we do know that we are "heirs of God and co-heirs with Christ" (Romans 8:17). Our infinite God will not run out of ideas and will have plenty of assignments for us to do.

When D. L. Moody lost everything in the Great Chicago Fire of 1871, an observer said to him, "You lost everything," and Moody said, "No, there's a great deal that I haven't lost." The man replied, "Oh, you're wealthy?" Moody replied, "No, no." Then he quoted, "He who overcomes shall inherit all things." And, as we know, Moody was right: "He that overcometh shall inherit all things; and I will be his God, and he shall be my son" (Revelation 21:7 KJV).

If your name is written in the Lamb's Book of Life there is nothing that can happen to you on this earth that will be of any permanent damage. You have a place reserved in heaven. There's a crown available that only you can wear. There's a room where only you can enter. There's an assignment that only you can perform. You will have direct access to the Father and the Son forever and ever.

YES, THE BIBLE BEGINS IN A GARDEN, BUT IT ENDS IN A CITY.

No wonder the hymn writer William Cowper wrote,

How thou can'st think so well of me
And be the God thou art
Is darkness to my intellect
But sunshine to my heart.

DOING LIFE TOGETHER IN THE NEW JERUSALEM

Why would the New Jerusalem need gates and walls? Needless to say, security in heaven should not be a problem. And it isn't. If we read the entire description of the city, we will discover that the text explicitly says that the gates will never be closed. There will be easy access for those who wish to travel wherever God sends them. Perhaps we will reign on other planets, or we will be involved in space exploration so that we might better understand the grandeur and power of God. The reason for the walls and gates is simply to affirm that this is indeed a city which can best represent the designs and purposes of God.

Yes, the Bible begins in a garden—the Garden of Eden—but it ends in a city. Why not a farm? Or a garden? A city represents community. For years, my wife, Rebecca, and I lived in a condo building, and it seemed as if the only time we would meet our neighbors would be when we were walking through the common areas, such as the entrance or the hallways. In the New Jerusalem, there will be plenty of "common areas," and we will not only connect with others, but delight in doing so. After all, we will be meeting a much larger family, and we need to have shared areas where we can talk and fellowship together.

Your mother will be known in heaven as your mother and you will undoubtedly remember your life on earth together (the same, of course, goes for your father, your children, and all your family and loved ones). At the same time, the kind of intimacy you have with your mother and your larger family on earth—those kinds of relationships will now be expanded to include all the people of God. We will spend **WE WILL NOT EVEN NEED FAITH, FOR FAITH WILL HAVE TURNED TO SIGHT.** eternity *together*. I expect that we will do projects together, worship together, eat together, and enjoy each other. We will be citizens of the same city, and submitting to the same Master.

I am reminded of a little girl whose mother was reading her bedtime stories about Jesus from a Bible picture book. The next morning the daughter said, "Oh, Mommy, I dreamed about Jesus, and you know, He's so much better than the pictures." I can assure you that it's going to be so much better than the pictures—even better than the verbal portrait that is given to us in the book of Revelation. We won't need the written Scriptures, for we shall be in God's presence and all that this entails. We will not even need faith, for faith will have turned to sight. "For we know in part and we prophesy in part, but when perfection comes, the imperfect disappears. . . . Now we see but a poor reflection as in a mirror, then we shall see face to face. Now I know in part; then I shall know fully, even as I am fully known" (1 Corinthians 13:9–10, 12).

Meanwhile here on earth we are doing the best we can on our journey to the heavenly city. When we arrive in the New Jerusalem, we will then realize that death on earth was but a gateway to an eternity filled with indescribable praise and wonder.

WHO WILL BE THERE?

Now for the most important question for each of us personally: Who will be there? These people will *not* be there: "But the cowardly, the unbelieving, the vile, the murderers, the sexually immoral, those who practice magic arts, the idolaters and all liars—their place will be in the fiery lake of burning sulfur. This is the second death" (Revelation 21:8). Just think for a moment about those who are suffering outside the gates of this blessed Paradise.

Later in the text, this description is essentially repeated: "Outside are the dogs, those who practice magic arts, the sexually immoral, the murderers, the idolaters and everyone who loves and practices falsehood" (22:15). Back in November 2009, Tareq and Michaele Salahi of Virginia, though uninvited, were cleverly able to enter the White House and attend a party hosted by the president. In fact, they were able to shake hands with both him and the vice president! This breach of security was a great embarrassment to our Secret Service, that elite corps committed to protecting the White House. There will be no gate-crashers in the New Jerusalem. If you are not on the list (the Lamb's Book of Life), there will be no entry. The heavenly city is guarded by the King Himself.

Think back to the descriptive list of all those who are described as being outside the city: "dogs"—that is those who are immoral—occult magicians, murderers, idolaters, and the like. Will these sins actually bar a person from entering the gate of heaven? Here is the best news you will ever hear: many people who committed these sins and worse will actually be in heaven!

Why can I say this? Because the real issue is whether we have had our robes washed in the blood of the Lamb:

"Behold, I am coming soon! My reward is with me, and I will give to everyone according to what he has done. I am the Alpha and the Omega, the First and the Last, the Beginning and the End. Blessed are those who wash their robes, that they may have the right to the tree of life and may go through the gates into the city" (22:12–14).

The issue really is not the greatness of your sin, however terrible it might be. God is able to take care of that. The issue is whether or not we have had our robes washed by Jesus, and whether we are clothed in His righteousness and not your own. Thankfully, this gift of righteousness is a free gift. Let's notice how the book of Revelation ends: "The Spirit and the bride say, 'Come!' And let him who hears say, 'Come!' Whoever is thirsty, let him come; and whoever wishes, let him take the free gift of the water of life" (22:17).

THE GOSPEL IS FOR THOSE WHO ARE THIRSTY.

If you've been told that you have to donate money to go to heaven, you have not heard the gospel. If you've been told that you must make yourself deserving to go to heaven, that is not the gospel. Nor is it through baptism, your church attendance, or through the sacraments.

The gospel is for those who are thirsty. We as sinners come without money, without price, to freely receive the gift of eternal life. Then we are able to enter into the city. But we must receive Christ while on earth; if we wait until after death it is too late. *The moment you die, your eternal future is irrevocably fixed.*

One day D. L. Moody said that he was listening very carefully when an old man stood up at a meeting and said, "It took me forty years to learn these three things." Moody thought, *If it took him forty years to learn this, maybe I can get a jump on things by listening carefully.* Then the man spoke, "Number one, I cannot earn my way to heaven. That's the first thing I learned. The second thing I learned is that God doesn't expect me to earn my way to heaven. God knows we can't. He knows it better than you do yourself. The third thing I learned is that Jesus did it all for those who believe in and trust Him.'"

Here is a poem I've often quoted:

The terrors of law and of God
With me can have nothing to do;
My Savior's obedience and blood
Hide all my transgressions from view.
My name on the palm of His hands
Eternity cannot erase;
Forever there it stands
A mark of indelible grace.

Three times in this last chapter Jesus says He is "coming soon" or suddenly (see vv. 7, 12, 20). After the last time Jesus says this, John himself adds, " Amen. Come, Lord Jesus. The grace of the Lord Jesus be with God's people. Amen" (vv. 20–21).

With these words, the New Testament comes to a fitting close. In effect, God Himself closes the book by affirming, "I have nothing more to say to you!"

And nor do I.

Let us watch and pray until He comes.

NOTES

1. Janet Willis, in her book *What on Earth Is Heaven Like?* (Greenville, SC: Ambassador International, 2011) gives extensive evidence that the size of the New Jerusalem will actually be much smaller than generally thought. She believes that in Revelation 21:16 John's reference to 12,000 stadia (approximately 1,380 miles) should be taken as a cubic number of stadia (or miles) rather than just a linear number because immediately after John gives the number, he follows with the phrase

"its length and width and height are equal." She bases her conclusions on the parallels between the New Jerusalem and Ezekiel's vision of the city on the Holy Allotment (Ezekiel 45:1–7; 48:30–35). Based on other Scriptures, she believes it will be a step-pyramid-shaped "structure like a city" (Ezekiel 40:2), with its base approximately eleven miles in length and width, and its height eleven miles. Thus the overall dimensions would equal 1,331 cubic miles. This city would then be the throne or the seat of Christ's government situated on a plateau centered where Jerusalem is today. Resurrected believers would be going in and out of the city on special assignments and the like.

Janet's intense interest in heaven came about after six of her children died in a horrific traffic accident in 1994. Whether or not her conclusions will be widely accepted remains to be seen, but after years of dedicated study, we are all helped and blessed by her intriguing insights regarding our future home.

CLOSING WORDS
ABOUT YOUR FUTURE

*More than at any other time in history, mankind
faces a crossroad. One path leads to despair and utter
hopelessness. The other to total extinction. Let us pray
that we have the wisdom to choose correctly.*
—Woody Allen

We smile at the pessimism of Woody Allen, but he is right in this regard: the world seems to be running out of good options economically and morally. No matter what our leaders do, there is a widespread sense that we are headed in the wrong direction, and one day we might wake up to discover that the world as we once knew it is gone. And of course, even if the world should continue in its present state for generations to come, someday all of us will find ourselves staring death in the face. Individually, we are at a crossroads: either we will prepare for eternity or we will find ourselves on the wrong side of the parted curtain.

The fact that Jesus will return to earth is as certain as the fact that He was born in Bethlehem, suffered and died on a cross, and was resurrected. The fact that He has not yet come should not deter us from preparing for His arrival. His delay is not denial, nor should His patience be interpreted as indifference.

The apostle Peter knew that there would be skeptics who would ridicule the second coming, arguing that since Jesus has not come after such a long time, it is quite certain He will not come at all. He warns, "First of all, you must understand that in the last days scoffers will come, scoffing and following their own evil desires. They will say, 'Where is this "coming" he promised? Ever since our fathers died, everything goes on as it has since the beginning of creation'" (2 Peter 3:3–4).

The delay of the Lord is neither a sign of God's disinterest nor His lack of resolve to fulfill His Word. Rather, Peter continues, "The Lord is not slow in keeping his promise, as some understand slowness. He is patient with you, not wanting anyone to perish, but everyone to come to repentance" (v. 9). That is to say, the delay in Christ's return is so that others who have not yet believed might do so. The door of opportunity is still open because the number that God intends to save is not yet complete.

In other words, among the reasons why the Lord has not come might be the fact that you, dear reader, are not yet ready for His return! What appears to be an indictment of the Lord's faithfulness is actually an invitation to receive the Lord's graciousness. As the writer of Hebrew says, "Today, if you hear his voice, do not harden your hearts as you did in the rebellion, during the time of testing in the desert" (3:7–8).

Peter then launches into one of the most dramatic and chilling descriptions of the Lord's return. This passage, though quoted earlier in this book, deserves being repeated. "But the day of the Lord will come like a thief. The heavens will disappear with a roar; the elements will be destroyed by fire, and the earth and everything in it will be laid bare" (2 Peter 3:10).

Peter continues to describe a day when all of our toys will be put back into the box, a day when everything we have ever accumulated will be subjected to the flames; a day when that which meant most to us on earth will be exposed, examined, and used to either validate or judge our lives. He writes, "Since everything will be destroyed in this way, what kind of people ought you to be? You ought to live holy and godly lives as you look forward to the day of God and speed its coming. That day will bring about the destruction of the heavens by fire, and the elements will melt in the heat" (vv. 11–12)

Houses, cars, bank accounts, jewelry, books—everything will be burned up. Chicago with its admired architecture; Rome with its magnificent history; New York with its skyscrapers; London with its opulence will be no more. Everything that you and I have ever known or owned will be gone.

What survives the raging fire? God, angels, demons, and people will live forever. As indicated earlier in this book, the world will be re-created in preparation of eternity. But the old order that you and I know and understand will never return. Only eternal beings will survive.

Enough has been said in this book to encourage you to prepare for that day through faith in Christ, who stands between us and God's rightful judgment against us. If you have never trusted Christ as Savior, here is a prayer you can use to make that transfer of trust:

God, I know I have sinned and apart from Your mercy I am headed for judgment. I admit that this judgment is deserved, for not only have I actively sinned, but in neglecting You, I have added to my own future condemnation.

But now I see that Jesus is not only a wonderful teacher, but also a wonderful Savior. I transfer my trust to Him at this moment. I understand that my eternal destiny rests with what He did in His death and resurrection for sinners such as I am. So, I repudiate any trust in my good works, my baptism, or my attempts at being moral or religious. I now know that all of that is like trash in Your holy presence.

I receive the promise of eternal life that is given to me in Your Holy Word. "Yet to all who received him, to those who believed in his name, he gave the right to become children of God—children born not of natural descent, nor of human decision or a husband's will, but born of God" (John 1:12–13).

Through Your Holy Spirit, give me the assurance that I now belong to You; to grow in my faith and give You glory for the rest of my life.

> *In Jesus' name,*
> *Amen.*

"You also must be ready, for the Son of Man is coming at an hour you do not expect" (Luke 12:40 ESV).

ALSO AVAILABLE FROM ERWIN W. LUTZER

S mall groups can now grapple with the content of *The King is Coming* together through this new study guide experience. Split into ten easily managed sections, the study guide will help participants explore and discover what comes next, while the DVD provides supplementary teachings for a full small group experience as participants begin to explore the end.

With summary questions, discussion points, and personal reflection, *The King is Coming Study Guide* and DVD will provide answers for those questioning what comes next—and empower and instruct them to live accordingly in the here and now.

moodypublishers.com

MOODY
Publishers™

From the Word to Life